St. Martin's Griffin
New York

NATURAL NURSERY KNITS

Twenty hand-knit projects for the new baby

ERIKA KNIGHT

photography by Kristin Perers

INTRODUCTION

This book always promised to be a pleasure to write. It brings together two of my passions—knitting for tiny babies and natural yarns. What better occasion is there to go eco-friendly than at the beginning of a new life? We all want to make what we believe to be the best choices for our children's well-being, so when it comes to choosing yarns for knitting for your baby, select authentic natural fibers whenever possible.

Nothing evokes fond memories of childhood so vividly as a pair of tiny baby booties, a quintessential teddy bear, or a cozy first blanket. This collection of nostalgic nursery knits is designed to welcome a newborn into the world—from dainty baby shoes and an adorably simple layette to luxuriously soft blankets, a pillow, and characterful soft toys that are destined to become toy box favorites.

Made from beautiful, natural, and sustainable yarns and trims, all of the projects are knitted in simple stitches and incorporate small design details that make a practical difference, like the integral scratch mittens on the nightie (see pages 72 and 73).

Of course, once baby has outgrown the knitwear, it can be washed, pressed, and put away for your next baby or passed on to a relative, friend, or neighbor. As generations have done before with their baby clothes, this is just simple, natural recycling. It's very reassuring to know that what you knit is not only kind to baby but is also gentle on the earth. Lovingly knitted, each piece you make is sure to become a keepsake of the future.

NATURAL YARNS

Derived from either animal or plant sources, natural yarns tend to have unique properties that give each project a particular character. I prefer to use baby animal fibers, such as alpaca and cashmere, for their natural softness and inherent luxury. However, other favorites include organic plant fibers, such as cotton and hemp, that are free from pesticides and chemical fertilizers. All these natural yarns absorb moisture and allow the skin to breathe, while remaining soft and comfortable to wear. When one invests time, dedication, and love into every stitch in excited anticipation of an impending new life, using natural yarns is so worthwhile.

BABY ALPACA

This luxurious fiber rivals cashmere and has less of a propensity to pill. With a beautiful drape, subtle sheen, and extreme softness, it glides through the fingers, so is great for hand knitting. Due to its hollow fibers and microscopic air pockets, pure alpaca is completely thermal. It retains warmth, is breathable, and absorbs moisture, making it an ideal choice for baby blankets and cardigans. Alpaca comes in a large number of natural shades, from white through beiges and grays to rich browns. A truly noble natural yarn.

BAMBOO

Bamboo yarn is derived from a grass that is harvested and distilled into cellulose, which is then spun into a yarn. A renewable and sustainable resource, bamboo thrives with no need for any pesticides or artificial fertilizers. It is harvested without killing the plant, and it only is a few months before it is ready to be harvested again. All this makes bamboo a very eco-friendly yarn. Pure bamboo fiber is biodegradable and naturally antibacterial. It is cool to wear, taking moisture away from the skin and allowing it to breathe. Bamboo yarn has a wonderful drape and natural sheen; next to your skin, it feels similar to silk and so it is a perfect choice when knitting baby's welcome blanket. Garments made from bamboo are luxuriously soft, smooth, and comfortable.

COTTON

Cotton grown organically is a natural vegetable fiber free from pesticides and artificial fertilizers, and one that is approved by a recognized regulating and certifying body. The organic cotton I prefer to use is fully certified; traceable all the way from seed to yarn store. Furthermore, the farmers are paid a living wage for its cultivation. Organic cotton is of a higher quality than conventional cotton; longer fibers result in softer but more durable and absorbent fabric. For a baby's delicate, sensitive skin, when the gentlest natural material is called for, organic cotton is the perfect choice.

MILK COTTON

Milk cotton is an extraordinarily soft yarn, which is so-called because it contains 30 percent milk protein. To produce the yarn, milk is dehydrated and skimmed, after which the milk protein casein is extracted. Once the protein is fluidized, it can then be spun and blended with other fibers, such as cotton. The result is an extremely smooth and fluid yarn that drapes and takes color well—a lovely yarn for nursery projects, especially tiny shoes and bonnets.

HEMP

Hemp is a perfect yarn for hand knitting: 100 percent natural with a dry handle, subtle sheen, and natural drape. Cool in summer, repelling 90 percent of UVA rays, and warm in winter, it keeps the wearer comfortable at all times. It is a robust fiber that gets softer each time it is washed. Hemp is the world's leading renewable resource; it can grow in virtually any soil and climate. It is excellent for reclaiming otherwise unusable land, and as it is unpalatable to insects, it requires no pesticides. Knitting with hemp requires a little adjustment and slightly more time because, like linen, hemp has no natural elasticity. Traditional methods of blocking and steaming, however, enhance the appearance and softness of the finished fabric and create a truly timeless piece.

PLANT AND HERB DYES

Color is an enormously important factor to consider when selecting natural yarns for babies. The naturally occurring colors of fibers can be very beautiful, especially those of baby alpaca and rare sheep breeds wools. Naturally marled, such yarns vary from ecru through soft gray to vicuna brown. With a yarn like alpaca, you can be reassured that no bleach, chemicals, or mordants have been used, which might irritate baby's skin or exacerbate any allergies. Elsewhere I have chosen organic cottons that are naturally dyed using plants and herbs, which produce no toxicity, just subtle pretty colors.

Organically grown cotton yarn is colored with sustainable natural dyes. Likewise, the dyeing process is sustainable and harms neither the environment nor the people who depend upon it. Only natural plant and herb dyes are used, which produce no toxic effluent and to keep them chemical-free there are no mordants. Instead, the natural dye stuffs are fixed onto the fiber by the addition of salt alone. Due to their organic nature, you will find there is some color variation in each shade, but this simply adds to the yarn's unique beauty.

To ensure the longevity of any naturally dyed yarn, avoid prolonged exposure to direct sunlight and follow the recommended garment care instructions. These natural variations do not in any way affect the quality or efficiency of the product.

ANNATTO (LIPSTICK TREE)

A red dye from the pulp of a fruit indigenous to the Caribbean and Central and South America. It is also used for coloring dairy products and confectionery, and was once used to treat fevers and kidney disease.

LOGWOOD

A chipped and fermented wood grown in tropical America, which is used in violet, blue, gray, and black dyes. A mild astringent, it is also used in treating chronic dysentery.

MADDER

A prickly herb from southern Europe grown as animal fodder, but whose roots can be powdered and used to produce many shades of red, pink, lilac, purple, brown, orange, and black. It is reputed to ease cases of jaundice.

BRAZILWOOD

A New World heartwood that revolutionized the world of sixteenth-century fashion with a true red dye the color of burning coals and gave birth to a nation.

YELLOWWOOD/CUBAWOOD

Trees with a yellow heart wood, used for dyeing browns, black, and yellows. The bark can be used in a gargle for sore throats.

QUEBRACHO

Tall evergreen tree from South America with particularly dense "axebreaker" wood that is a natural source of tannin. Can be used to help in cases of asthma and emphysema.

NATURAL NURSERY COLLECTION

CELLULAR BLANKET
see pages 78–79

TEDDY BEAR
see pages 80–83

INITIALED WASHCLOTH
see pages 84–87

CLASSIC CARDIGAN
see pages 88–89

HARE DOORSTOP
see pages 90–93

SACHET COVER
see pages 94–95

RABBIT RATTLE
see pages 96–97

HAT AND BOOTS
see pages 98–99

FAIR ISLE BUNTING
see pages 100–101

FIRST BLANKET
see pages 102–103

DRESS AND PANTIES
see pages 104–107

RECYCLED-RAG BASKET
see pages 108–109

SWEATER AND PANTS
see pages 110–113

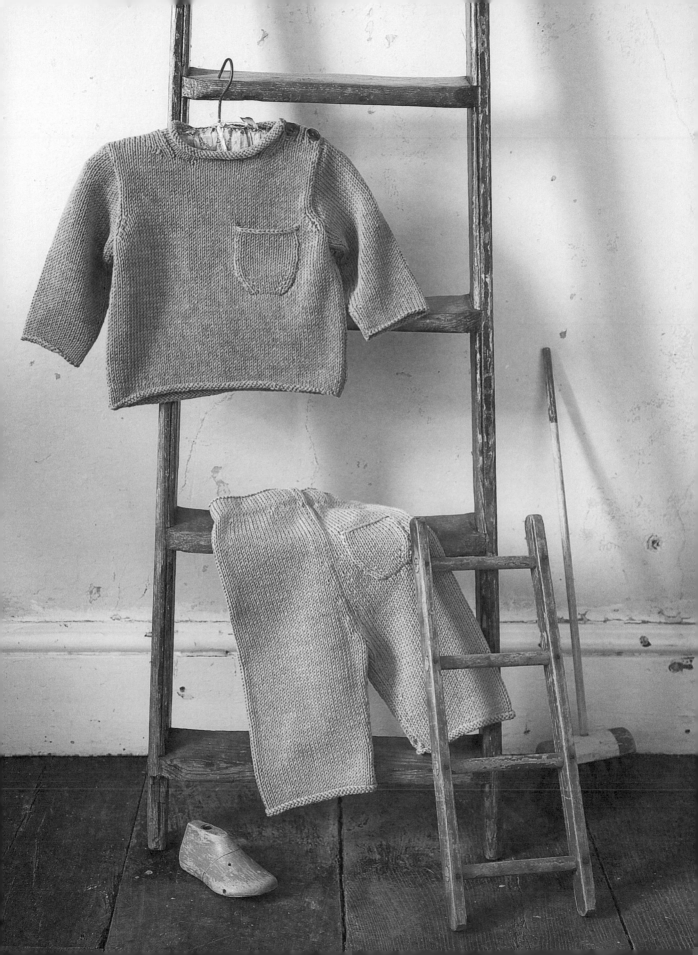

BOOTIES AND BONNET
see pages 114–117

LACE PILLOW
see pages 118–119

BIRD MOBILE
see pages 120–121

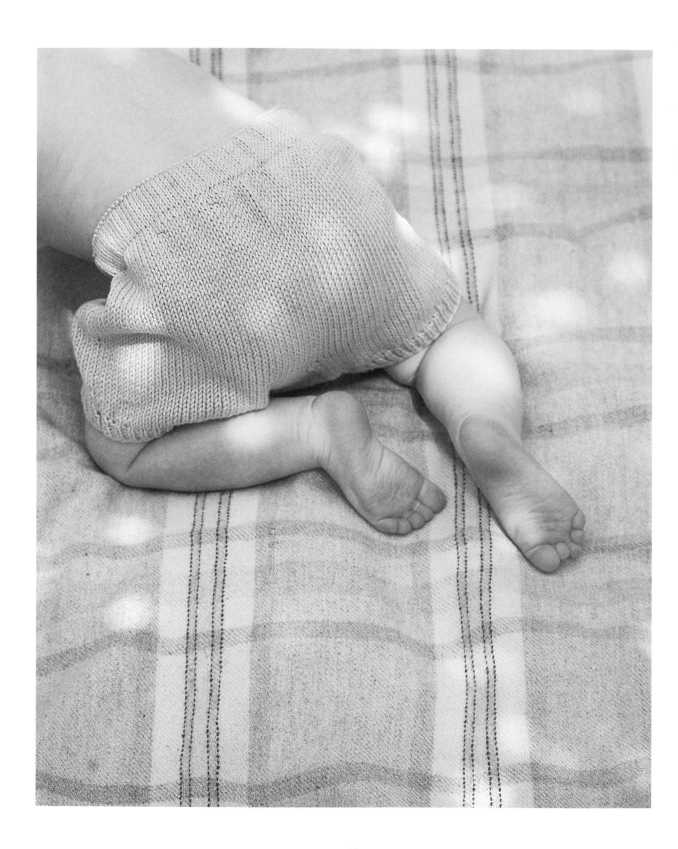

DIAPER COVER
see pages 122–123

HEIRLOOM CRIB QUILT
see pages 124–127

SPOTTY GIRAFFE
see pages 128–129

NIGHTIE AND HAT
see pages 130–132

NATURAL NURSERY PATTERNS

CELLULAR BLANKET

see pages 14–17

Knit this classic blanket as a welcome gift for a newborn baby. With a decorative open-stitch center contrasted by a simple selvage border, the cellular construction is both insulating and breathable, making it very comfortable for baby. The milk cotton yarn has a beautiful sheen and drape, which enhances the stitch texture. The instructions given here are for the perfect size blanket for a Moses basket or for baby to cuddle into, but it can be easily made larger to suit a crib or a bed— simply cast on more stitches in multiples of four and add extra rows of the pattern.

SIZE
Approximately 26¾in/68cm x 35½in/90cm

MATERIALS
7 x 1¾oz/50g balls (124yd/113m per ball) of Rowan Milk Cotton DK (or a similar double-knitting-weight cotton-blend yarn) in pink
Pair of size 5 (3.75mm) knitting needles

GAUGE
21 sts and 28 rows to 4in/10cm square over cell st patt using size 5 (3.75mm) needles. Always work a gauge swatch and change needle size if necessary.

ABBREVIATIONS
See page 139.

TO MAKE
Cast on 169 sts and work in rib as follows:
Rib row 1 (RS) K1, [p1, k1] to end of row.
Rib row 2 P1, [k1, p1] to end of row.
Rep last 2 rows until work measures 2½in/6.5cm, ending with RS facing for next row.
Cont in cell st patt with ribbed side borders as follows:
Row 1 (RS) [K1, p1] 12 times, k3, *yo, sl 1, k2tog, psso, yo, k1; rep from * to last 26 sts, k2, [p1, k1] 12 times.
Row 2 [P1, k1] 12 times, p to last 24 sts, [k1, p1] 12 times.
Row 3 [K1, p1] 12 times, k2, k2tog, yo, k1, *yo, sl 1, k2tog, psso, yo, k1; rep from * to last 28 sts, yo, skp, k2, [p1, k1] 12 times.
Row 4 Rep row 2.
Last 4 rows are repeated to form cell st patt with ribbed side borders.
Cont in patt as set until work measures 33in/83.5cm from cast-on edge, ending with RS facing for next row.
Rib row 1 (RS) K1, [p1, k1] to end of row.
Rib row 2 P1, [k1, p1] to end of row.
Rep last 2 rows for 2½in/6.5cm.
Bind off loosely in rib.

TO FINISH
Weave in any yarn ends.
Lay work out flat and gently steam.

TEDDY BEAR

see pages 18–19

No nursery is complete without the traditional child's teddy bear. Knitted in garter stitch with natural British sheep breeds wool and with one foot pad, paw pad, and inner ear of cotton fabric, this teddy bear can easily be customized to coordinate with baby's nursery.

SIZE
Approximately 14¼in/36cm tall

MATERIALS
3 x 3½oz/100g balls (120yd/110m per ball) of Rowan Purelife British Sheep Breeds Undyed (or a similar aran-weight wool yarn) in gray-brown (A) and a small amount of mid brown (B), OR R.E. Dickie British Breeds Aran Weight Natural in brown-cream marl (A) and a small amount of dark brown (B)
Pair of size 6 (4mm) knitting needles
Natural organic cotton stuffing
2 buttons with shanks for eyes
Strong thread for movable joints
Templates for foot and paw pads and inner ear (see page 134)
Fabric scraps, approximately 12in/30cm square, for foot and paw pads and inner ear
Contrasting yarn for nose and mouth embroidery
Fabric strip or ribbon for neck tie

GAUGE
22 sts and 40 rows to 4in/10cm square over garter stitch, before stuffing, using size 6 (4mm) needles. Always work a gauge swatch and change needle size if necessary.

ABBREVIATIONS
kfb knit into front and back of next stitch to increase one stitch.
See also page 139.

TIPS AND TECHNIQUES
* The teddy bear is worked throughout in garter stitch (knit every row) using size 6 (4mm) needles.
* When working k2tog, keep your yarn tension tight to avoid any holes.
* In the following instructions one of each of the pairs of foot pads, inner ears, and paw pads are knitted and one of each are made with fabric (see templates on page 134), but if you prefer, you can knit them all or make them all with fabric.
* Use a small amount of fabric glue where the nose is to be stitched, this helps prevent the threads from slipping.

BODY (MAKE ONE)
The body is worked from the lower edge to the neck edge.
With A, cast on 18 sts.
Rows 1 and 2 K.
Row 3 Kfb, k7, [kfb] twice, k7, kfb. **22 sts.**
Row 4 Kfb, k8, [kfb] 4 times, k8, kfb. **28 sts.**
Row 5 K.
Row 6 Kfb, k11, [kfb] 4 times, K11, kfb. **34 sts.**
Row 7 K.
Row 8 Kfb, k14, [kfb] 4 times, K14, kfb. **40 sts.**
Row 9 Kfb, k17, [kfb] 4 times, k17, kfb. **46 sts.**
Row 10 K.
Row 11 Kfb, k20, [kfb] 4 times, k20, kfb. **52 sts.**
Row 12 K.
Row 13 Kfb, k23, [kfb] 4 times, k23, kfb. **58 sts.**
K 10 rows.

Row 24 K2tog, k to last 2 sts, k2tog. 56 sts.
Row 25 K11, [k2tog] twice, k26, [k2tog] twice, k11. 52 sts.
Row 26 K.
Row 27 K24, [k2tog] twice, k24. 50 sts.
K 2 rows.
Row 30 K10, [k2tog] twice, k22, [k2tog] twice, k10. 46 sts.
Row 31 K21, [k2tog] twice, k21. 44 sts.
K 2 rows.
Row 34 K20, [k2tog] twice, k20. 42 sts.
Row 35 K.
Row 36 K19, [k2tog] twice, k19. 40 sts.
Row 37 K8, [k2tog] twice, k6, [k2tog] twice, k6, [k2tog] twice, k8. 34 sts.
Row 38 K.
Row 39 K15 sts, [k2tog] twice, k15. 32 sts.
Row 40 K8, k2tog, k4, [k2tog] twice, k4, k2tog, k8. 28 sts.
Row 41 K12, [k2tog] twice, k12. 26 sts.
Row 42 K6, k2tog, k3, [k2tog] twice, k3, k2tog, k6. 22 sts.
Row 43 K7, [k2tog] 4 times, k7. 18 sts.
Row 44 K2tog, k14, k2tog. 16 sts.
Row 45 K.
Row 46 K2tog, k12, k2tog. 14 sts.
Row 47 K.
Row 48 K2tog, k10, k2tog. 12 sts.
Row 49 [K2tog] 6 times. 6 sts.
Cut yarn, thread through rem sts, pull up tightly, and secure firmly.

HEAD (MAKE ONE)
With A, cast on 22 sts.
Rows 1 and 2 K.
Row 3 K8, kfb, k4, kfb, k8. 24 sts.
K 3 rows.
Row 7 K8, kfb, k6, kfb, k8. 26 sts.

Row 8 Cast on 2 sts onto left needle, k to end. 28 sts.
Row 9 Cast on 2 sts onto left needle, k to end. 30 sts.
Row 10 Cast on 2 sts onto left needle, k to end. 32 sts.
Row 11 Cast on 2 sts onto left needle, k to end. 34 sts.
Row 12 Kfb, k11, kfb, k8, kfb, k11, kfb. 38 sts.
K 3 rows.
Row 16 K13, kfb, k10, kfb, k13. 40 sts.
Row 17 Kfb, k to last st, kfb. 42 sts.
K 5 rows.
Row 23 K14, k2tog, k10, k2tog, k14. 40 sts.
Row 24 Bind off 7 sts, k to end. 33 sts.
Row 25 Bind off 7 sts, k to end. 26 sts.
Row 26 K2tog, k5, k2tog, k8, k2tog, k5, k2tog. 22 sts.
Row 27 K2tog, k4, k2tog, k6, k2tog, k4, k2tog. 18 sts.
Row 28 K2tog, k3, k2tog, k4, k2tog, k3, k2tog. 14 sts.
Row 29 [K2tog, k2] 3 times, k2tog. 10 sts.
Row 30 K2tog, k6, k2tog. 8 sts.
K 5 rows.
Row 36 K2tog, k4, k2tog. 6 sts.
K 4 rows.
Row 41 K2tog, k2, k2tog. 4 sts.
K 12 rows.
Bind off.

FOOT PAD (MAKE ONE)
With B, cast on 6 sts.
Row 1 K.
Rows 2, 3, and 4 Kfb, k to last st, kfb. 12 sts.
K 14 rows.
Row 19 K2tog, k8, k2tog. 10 sts.
K 13 rows.
Row 33 K2tog, k to last 2 sts, k2tog.
Row 34 K.
Rows 35–42 [Rep rows 33 and 34] 4 times.

Bind off.
(The other foot pad is made with fabric as explained in the finishing instructions.)

LEGS (MAKE TWO)
The leg is worked starting at the foot end.
With A, cast on 48 sts.
Rows 1–6 K.
Row 7 K18, [k2tog] 6 times, k18. 42 sts.
Row 8 K.
Row 9 K15, [k2tog] 6 times, k15. 36 sts.
Row 10 K.
Row 11 K12, [k2tog] 6 times, k12. 30 sts.
Row 12 K.
Row 13 K2tog, k7, [k2tog] 6 times, k7, k2tog. 22 sts.
Row 14 K.
Row 15 K5, [k2tog] 6 times, k5. 16 sts.
K 24 rows.
Row 40 Kfb, k6, [kfb] twice, k6, kfb. 20 sts.
Row 41 K.
Row 42 Kfb, k8, [kfb] twice, k8, kfb. 24 sts.
Rows 43 and 44 K.
Row 45 K2tog, k8, [k2tog] twice, k8, k2tog. 20 sts.
Row 46 K.
Row 47 K2tog, k6, [k2tog] twice, k6, k2tog. 16 sts.
Row 48 K2tog, k4, [k2tog] twice, k4, k2tog. 12 sts.
Row 49 K2tog, k2, [k2tog] twice, k2, k2tog. 8 sts.
Row 50 [K2tog] 4 times. 4 sts.
Row 51 [K2tog] twice. 2 sts.
Cut yarn, thread through rem sts, pull up tightly, and secure firmly.

OUTER EARS (MAKE TWO)
With A, cast on 10 sts.
Rows 1–10 K.
Row 11 K2tog, k6, k2tog. 8 sts.

K 1 row.
Row 13 K2tog, k4, k2tog. 6 sts.
K 1 row.
Bind off, working k2tog at each end of row.

INNER EAR (MAKE ONE)
With B, make exactly as for Outer Ear.
(The other inner ear is made with fabric as explained in the finishing instructions.)

ARMS (MAKE TWO)
The arm is worked starting at the paw end.
With A, cast on 4 sts.
Row 1 K.
Row 2 Kfb, k2, kfb. 6 sts.
K 3 rows.
Row 6 Kfb, k4, kfb. 8 sts.
K 3 rows.
Row 10 Kfb, k6, kfb. 10 sts.
SHAPE PAW
Row 11 K2tog, k to last st, kfb. 10 sts.
K 3 rows.
Row 15 K.
Row 16 K2tog, k to last st, kfb. 10 sts.
K 3 rows.**
Row 20 Cast on 10 sts onto left needle, k to end. 20 sts.
Row 21 K2tog, k7, [kfb] twice, k7, k2tog. 20 sts.
K 3 rows.
Row 25 K2tog, k7, [kfb] twice, k7. k2tog. 20 sts.
K 3 rows.
Row 29 K2tog, k7, [kfb] twice, k7, k2tog. 20 sts.
K 21 rows.
SHAPE TOP OF ARM
Row 51 K2tog, k6, [k2tog] twice, k6, k2tog. 16 sts.
K 2 rows.

Row 54 K2tog, k4, [k2tog] twice, k4, k2tog. 12 sts.
Rows 55 and 56 K.
Row 57 K2tog, k2, [k2tog] twice, k2, k2tog. 8 sts.
Row 58 [K2tog] 4 times. 4 sts.
Row 59 [K2tog] twice. 2 sts.
Row 60 K2tog.
Cut yarn, thread through last st, pull up tightly, and
secure firmly.

PAW PADS (MAKE TWO)
With B, make as for Arm to **, then bind off.

TO FINISH
Sew the body seam and head seam, stitching them
together firmly using small backstitches, but leave a
small opening for stuffing.
Cut a fabric foot pad, inner ear, and paw pad (see
page 134 for templates), making sure they are big
enough to match knitted versions plus a seam
allowance. (Ensure that you cut the fabric foot and
paw pads for the chosen limb, i. e., with right side of
fabric correct for right or left limb.) Set these fabric
pieces aside.
Sew leg and arm seams, using firm backstitches and
leaving a small opening for stuffing.
Sew knitted paw pad to one arm and fabric one to
the other. Do the same with the foot pads on the legs.
Stuff body, head, legs, and arms firmly, but avoid
distorting the limbs. Then stitch the openings closed.
Sew the head to the body using ladder stitch, which
can be drawn up tightly until the head is as firmly
secured as required.
Attach the limbs to the body with thread jointing,
using strong thread to make movable joints.
Attach the button eyes to the head using strong
thread as follows:

Pass two strands of thread together through the
button shank and tie securely to the shank at the
center of the strands. Thread the four thread ends
onto a blunt-ended yarn needle and insert through
the required eye position and out through the back
of the neck.
Unthread two of the four thread ends and make a
1/8in/3mm stitch with the remaining two strands.
Then unthread these two and tie securely to the first
two thread ends, pulling the eye into the head to the
desired depth. Knot several times and fasten off by
passing the thread ends inside the head before
cutting them.
Sew a knitted inner ear to one outer ear and a
fabric one to the other. Sew the ears to the head
using ladder stitch so you can pull them into the
required shape.
Embroider the nose and mouth using a contrasting
yarn.
Tie on ribbon or fabric-strip neck tie.

INITIALED WASHCLOTH

see pages 20–21

A simple washcloth, knitted in natural hemp yarn can be personalized with an initial worked in stockinette stitch on a reverse stockinette stitch ground. Wrapped up with a piece of handmade organic soap, this washcloth makes a practical yet inexpensive gift.

SIZE
Approximately 11¾in/30cm square

MATERIALS
1 x 3½oz/100g skein (165yd/150m per skein) of Lanaknits Allhemp6 (or a similar double-knitting-weight hemp yarn) in green
Pair of size 5 (3.75mm) knitting needles
Contrasting cotton embroidery thread (for optional blanket stitch edging)
6in/15cm of ⅝in/1.5cm wide cotton gingham ribbon and one snap (optional)

GAUGE
22 sts and 26 rows to 4in/10cm square over St st using size 5 (3.75mm) needles. Always work a gauge swatch and change needle size if necessary.

ABBREVIATIONS
See page 139.

TIPS AND TECHNIQUES
* Each letter is worked from a chart, 24 sts wide and 32 rows long, and is placed as given in the pattern instructions. See pages 85–87 for the complete set of alphabet charts and choose the letter you desire.
* Read each chart from right to left for the odd-numbered (RS) rows and from left to right for the even-numbered (WS) rows.
See page 87 for key.

TO MAKE
Cast on 66 sts.
P 2 rows.
Next row (RS) K2, p to last 2 sts, k2.
Next row K.
Rep last 2 rows 10 times more.
PLACE LETTER CHART
Row 1 (RS) K2, p19, work across 24 sts of 1st row of chart, p19, k2.
Row 2 K21, work across 24 sts of 2nd row of chart, k21.
Last 2 rows set the position of the chart and are repeated.
Cont as set foll the chart until all 32 chart rows have been completed and RS of work is facing for next row.
Beg with a RS row, work 21 rows more in reverse St st with garter st side borders as set, ending with WS facing for next row.
P 2 rows. Bind off.

TO FINISH
Weave in any yarn ends.
Lay work out flat and gently steam.
Leave the washcloth plain or work a blanket stitch edging around the outside edge using a contrasting cotton embroidery thread.
To make a hanging loop, thread the gingham ribbon through the washcloth, approximately 1¼in/3cm in from one corner, fold under the ends of the ribbon, and sew the snap in place to fasten the ends of the ribbon together.

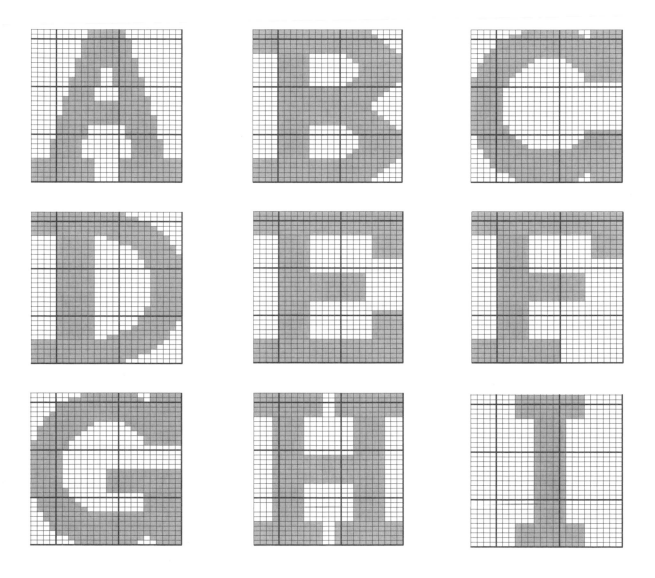

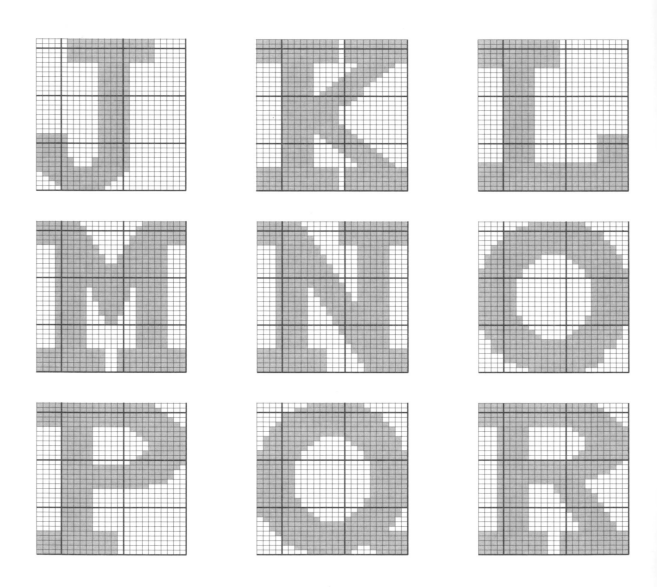

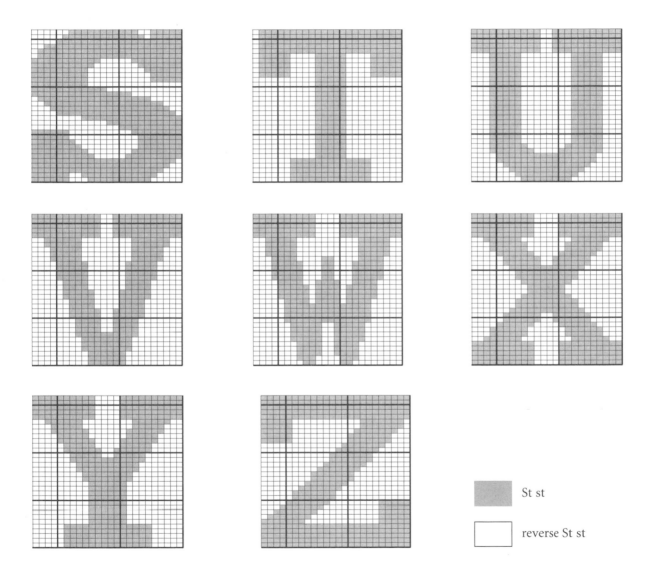

St st

reverse St st

CLASSIC CARDIGAN

see pages 22–23

Worked in one piece to ensure maximum ease for the knitter and comfort for the wearer, this simple cardigan is made in the softest baby-alpaca yarn. This design combines integral rib edgings and snap fastenings for a modern, practical touch.

SIZES
To fit newborn (0–3: 3–6) months
Knitted chest measurement 15 (17: 19¼)in/38 (43: 49)cm
Length from shoulder 7½ (8¼: 9)in/19 (21: 23)cm
Sleeve length 2¾ (3¼: 3½)in/7 (8: 9)cm

MATERIALS
2 (2: 3) x 1¾oz/50g balls (109yd/100m per ball) of Rowan Classic (RYC) Baby Alpaca DK (or a similar double-knitting-weight alpaca yarn) in cream, brown, or gray
Pair each of sizes 5 and 6 (3.75mm and 4mm) knitting needles
4 natural horn buttons (from a sustainable source)
4 snaps

GAUGE
22 sts and 30 rows to 4in/10cm square over St st using size 6 (4mm) needles. Always work a gauge swatch and change needle size if necessary.

ABBREVIATIONS
See page 139.

TO MAKE
The cardigan is made in one piece starting at the lower back edge.

BACK
With size 5 (3.75mm) needles, cast on 44 (50: 56) sts.
Row 1 (RS) K2, [p1, k2] to end of row.
Row 2 P2, [k1, p2] to end of row.
Rep last 2 rows twice more.
Change to size 6 (4mm) needles.
Beg with a k row, work in St st until back measures 4¼ (4¾: 5¼)in/10.5 (12: 13.5)cm from cast-on edge, ending with RS facing for next row.

SHAPE SLEEVES
Next row (RS) Cast on 18 (20: 22) sts loosely onto left needle, then work [p1, k2] twice, p1, k to end of row.
Next row Cast on 18 (20: 22) sts loosely onto left needle, then work [k1, p2] twice, k1, p to last 7 sts, [k1, p2] twice, k1. **80 (90: 100) sts.**
Work even in St st with rib borders as set until work measures 6¾ (7½: 8¼)in/17 (19: 21)cm from cast-on edge, ending with RS facing for next row.
Next row (RS) P1, [k2, p1] twice, k19 (21: 23), [p1, k2] 9 (11: 13) times, p1, k19 (21: 23), [p1, k2] twice, p1.
Next row K1, [p2, k1] twice, p19 (21: 23), [k1, p2] 9 (11: 13) times, k1, p19 (21: 23), [k1, p2] twice, k1.
Rep last 2 rows once more.

SHAPE RIGHT FRONT SLOPE AND SLEEVE
Next row (RS) P1, [k2, p1] twice, k19 (21: 23), [p1, k2] twice, p1, turn and leave rem sts on a holder.
Next row K1, [p2, k1] twice, p19 (21: 23), [k1, p2] twice, k1.
Next row (inc row) P1, [k2, p1] twice, k to last 9 sts, m1, k2, [p1, k2] twice, p1.
Inc 1 st at neck edge as set on every foll alt row until there are 44 (44: 46) sts.

Inc 1 st at neck edge as set on every row until there
are – (49: 54) sts.
ALL SIZES
Work even until sleeve measures 6¾ (7: 7½)in/
17 (18: 19)cm in width, ending at cuff edge.
Bind off 18 (20: 22) sts at beg of next row. **26 (29: 32) sts.**
Work even until work measures 14¼ (15¾: 17¼)in/
36 (40: 44)cm from cast-on edge, ending with RS
facing for next row and inc 1 st at end of last row.
27 (30: 33) sts.
Change to size 5 (3.75mm) needles and work in rib
as follows:
Row 1 (RS) [K2, p1] to end of row.
Row 2 [K1, p2] to end of row.
Rep last 2 rows twice more.
Bind off in rib.
With size 6 (4mm) needles and RS facing, rejoin yarn
to rem sts, bind off 14 (20: 26) sts at center back in
rib, rib next 6 sts as set, k to last 7 sts, p1, [k2, p1] to
end of row.

SHAPE LEFT FRONT SLOPE AND SLEEVE
Next row (WS) K1, [p2, k1] twice, p19 (21: 23),
[k1, p2] twice, k1.
Next row (inc row) P1, [k2, p1] twice, k2, m1, k to
last 7 sts, [p1, k2] twice, p1.
Inc 1 st at neck edge as set on every foll alt row until
there are 44 (44: 46) sts.
2ND AND 3RD SIZES ONLY
Inc 1 st at neck edge as set on every row until there
are – (49: 54) sts.
ALL SIZES
Work even until sleeve measures 6¾ (7: 7½)in/
17 (18: 19)cm in width, ending at cuff edge.
Bind off 18 (20: 22) sts at beg of next row.

26 (29: 32) sts.
Work even until work measures 14¼ (15¾: 17¼)in/
36 (40: 44)cm from cast-on edge, ending with RS
facing for next row and inc 1 st at beg of last row.
27 (30: 33) sts.
Change to size 5 (3.75mm) needles and work in rib
as follows:
Row 1 (RS) [P1, k2] to end of row.
Row 2 [P2, k1] to end of row.
Rep last 2 rows twice more.
Bind off in rib.

POCKETS (MAKE 2)
With size 5 (3.75mm) needles, cast on 11 sts.
Beg with a k row, work 2 rows in St st.
Next row K3, m1, k to last 3 sts, m1, k3. **13 sts.**
P 1 row.
Rep last 2 rows once more. **15 sts.**
Work even for 8 rows, ending with RS facing for
next row.
Work 2 rows in rib as follows:
Row 1 K1, [p1, k2] to last 2 sts, p1, k1.
Row 2 P1, [k1, p2], to last 2 sts, k1, p1.
Bind off in rib.

TO FINISH
Weave in any yarn ends.
Lay work out flat and gently steam.
Sew side and sleeve seams.
Sew on pockets.
Sew snaps to ribbed front bands, then sew buttons
above snaps to detail.

HARE DOORSTOP

see pages 24–25

A practical and adorable doorstop for the nursery, this sitting hare is knitted in stockinette stitch with natural hemp yarn. One floppy ear acts as a handle, and the hare is stuffed with organic cotton and natural rice grains for ballast.

SIZE
Approximately 13¾in/35cm from tip of ear to base

MATERIALS
1 x 3½oz/100g skein (165yd/150m per skein) of Lanaknits Allhemp6 (or a similar double-knitting-weight hemp yarn) in ecru
Pair of size 3 (3.25mm) knitting needles
½yd/50cm of muslin for lining
Dry rice (or small dry lentils) for stuffing
Organic cotton stuffing
Small piece of cardboard
Small amount of mid-brown yarn for pompom tail

GAUGE
22 sts and 30 rows to 4in/10cm square over St st using size 3 (3.25mm) needles. Always work a gauge swatch and change needle size if necessary.

ABBREVIATIONS
See page 139.

TIPS AND TECHNIQUES
* When you have made and checked your gauge swatch, unravel it and use the yarn to work the base—if you do not, you may need an extra skein.
* Both a chart and written instruction are given for Sides 1 and 2; choose whichever method you prefer.

* If working from the chart work, for Side 1 read odd-numbered knit rows from right to left and even-numbered purl rows from left to right. For Side 2, read in the same direction, but purl odd-numbered rows and knit even-numbered rows.
* Work all increases by working into the front and back of the same stitch, one stitch in from the edge.
* Work all decreases one stitch in from the edge as well, working k2tog or p2tog on Side 1; and k2tog tbl or p2tog tbl on Side 2.

SIDES 1 AND 2
Sides 1 and 2 are made in the same way, but beg Side 1 with a k row and beg Side 2 with a p row.
Cast on 45 sts and work in St st as follows:
Rows 1 and 2 Work 2 rows.
Row 3 Inc 1 st at end of row. 46 sts.
Row 4 Work 1 row.
Row 5 Inc 1 st at end of row. 47 sts.
Row 6 Work 1 row.
Row 7 Dec 1 st at beg of row. 46 sts.
Row 8 Work 1 row.
Row 9 Dec 1 st at beg and inc 1 st at end of row. 46 sts.
Row 10 Dec 1 st at end of row. 45 sts.
Row 11 Bind off 3 sts at beg of row. 42 sts.
Row 12 Dec 1 st at end of row. 41 sts.
Row 13 Bind off 2 sts at beg and dec 1 st at end of row. 38 sts.
Row 14 Bind off 3 sts at beg and dec 1 st at end of row. 34 sts.
Row 15 Dec 1 st at end of row. 33 sts.
Row 16 Work 1 row.
Row 17 Dec 1 st at beg of row. 32 sts.
Row 18 Inc 1 st at beg of row. 33 sts.
Row 19 Work 1 row.
Row 20 Inc 1 st at beg of row. 34 sts.

Rows 21 and 22 Work 2 rows.
Row 23 Inc 1 st each end of row. 36 sts.
Row 24 Inc 1 st at end of row. 37 sts.
Row 25 Inc 1 st at beg of row. 38 sts.
Row 26 Inc 1 st at beg of row. 39 sts.
Row 27 Inc 1 st at beg of row. 40 sts.
Row 28 and 29 Work 2 rows.
Row 30 Inc 1 st at beg of row. 41 sts.
Row 31 Inc 1 st at beg of row. 42 sts.
Rows 32 and 33 Work 2 rows.
Row 34 Inc 1 st at end of row. 43 sts.
Rows 35, 36, and 37 Work 3 rows.
Rows 38 Dec 1 st at beg of row and inc 1 st at end of row. 43 sts.
Row 39 Work 1 row.
Row 40 Dec 1 st at beg of row. 42 sts.
Row 41 Inc 1 st at beg of row and dec 1 st at end of row. 42 sts.
Row 42 Work 1 row.
Row 43 Dec 1 st at end of row. 41 sts.
Row 44 Work 1 row.
Row 45 Inc 1 st at beg of row and dec 1 st at end of row. 41 sts.
Row 46 Dec 1 st at beg of row. 40 sts.
Row 47 Dec 1 st at end of row. 39 sts.
Row 48 Dec 1 st at beg of row. 38 sts.
Row 49 Cast on 5 sts at beg of row and dec 1 st at end of row. 42 sts.
Row 50 Dec 1 st at beg of row and inc 1 st at end of row. 42 sts.
Row 51 Inc 1 st at beg of row and dec 1 st at end of row. 42 sts.
Row 52 Dec 1 st at beg of row and inc 1 st at end of row. 42 sts.
Row 53 Dec 1 st at end of row. 41 sts.
Row 54 Dec 1 st at beg of row. 40 sts.

Row 55 Dec 1 st at end of row. 39 sts.
Row 56 Bind off 4 sts at beg of row. 35 sts.
Row 57 Dec 1 st at end of row. 34 sts.
Row 58 Bind off 4 sts at beg of row. 30 sts.
Row 59 Dec 1 st at each end of row. 28 sts.
Row 60 Bind off 3 sts at beg of row. 25 sts.
Row 61 Dec 1 st at end of row. 24 sts.
Row 62 Bind off 2 sts at beg of row and dec 1 st at end of row. 21 sts.
Row 63 Dec 1 st each end of row. 19 sts.
Row 64 Bind off 2 sts at beg of row. 17 sts.
Row 65 Dec 1 st each end of row. 15 sts.
Row 66 Dec 1 st at beg of row. 14 sts.
Row 67 Dec 1 st at beg of row. 13 sts.
Row 68 Dec 1 st at end of row. 12 sts.
Row 69 Dec 1 st at beg of row and inc 1 st at end of row. 12 sts.
Row 70 Dec 1 st at end of row. 11 sts.
Row 71 Dec 1 st at beg of row and inc 1 st at end of row. 11 sts.
Row 72 Work 1 row.
Row 73 Inc 1 st at end of row. 12 sts.
Row 74 Inc 1 st at beg of row and dec 1 st at end of row. 12 sts.
Row 75 Work 1 row.
Row 76 Inc 1 st at beg of row and dec 1 st at end of row. 12 sts.
Row 77 Inc 1 st at end of row. 13 sts.
Row 78 Dec 1 st at end of row. 12 sts.
Row 79 Work 1 row.
Row 80 Inc 1 st at beg of row and dec 1 st at end of row. 12 sts.
Rows 81 and 82 Work 2 rows.
Row 83 Inc 1 st at end of row. 13 sts.
Row 84 Dec 1 st at end of row. 12 sts.
Rows 85 and 86 Work 2 rows.

Row 87 Inc 1 st at end of row. 13 sts.
Rows 88 and 89 Work 2 rows.
Row 90 Dec 1 st at end of row. 12 sts.
Row 91 Inc 1 st at end of row. 13 sts.
Rows 92 and 93 Work 2 rows.
Row 94 Dec 1 st at end of row. 12 sts.
Row 95 Work 1 row.
Row 96 Dec 1 st at end of row. 11 sts.
Row 97 Dec 1 st at beg of row. 10 sts.
Row 98 Dec 1 st each end of row. 8 sts.
Row 99 Work 1 row.
Row 100 Dec 1 st at end of row. 7 sts.
Row 101 Dec 1 st at beg of row. 6 sts.
Row 102 Dec 1 st each end of row. 4 sts.
Row 103 Dec 1 st at beg of row. 3 sts.
Row 104 Work 3 sts tog.
Fasten off.

BASE (MAKE ONE)
Cast on 4 sts and beg with a k row, work in St st
as follows:
Inc 1 st at each end of 3rd row and every foll alt row
until there are 20 sts.
Work even for 25 rows, so ending with RS facing for
next row.
Dec 1 st at each end of next row and every foll alt
rows until 4 sts rem.
Work 1 row.
Bind off.

OUTER EARS (MAKE TWO)
Cast on 17 sts.
For first outer ear, beg with a k row, work from row
65 of instructions for Sides to end.
For second outer ear, but beg with a p row, work
from row 65 of instructions for Sides to end.

TO MAKE INNER LINING
Lay one Side piece and the Base on paper and draw
around each piece (excluding ears), adding ½in/1cm
all around each piece for seam allowances. Cut out
these paper templates and use them to cut two side
pieces and one base piece from the lining fabric.
Sew the two lining side pieces together around back,
head, and front of hare shape.
Cut one base piece in cardboard.
Stuff head and top of hare fully with organic stuffing.
Pour in rice on top of the stuffing to fill inner lining
and provide a firm base for the doorstop.
Sew on lining base, leaving an opening, then insert
cardboard into base and stitch opening closed.

TAIL (MAKE ONE)
Cut two circles of cardboard 2in/5cm in diameter
and cut a hole in the center of each circle.
Thread a blunt-ended yarn needle with yarn.
Holding the circles together, wind the yarn
continually through the center and around outer
edges of the circles until the hole has closed.
Insert tip of scissors between the two circles and cut
the yarn around the edge of the cardboard circles.
Tie a piece of yarn tightly between the two cardboard
circles around the yarn strands. Remove the cardboard.
Trim any uneven strands for a neat finish.

TO FINISH
Weave in any yarn ends.
Lay knitting out flat and gently steam.
Sew one outer ear to each knitted Side piece and stuff
each ear with organic cotton. Sew the sides of the
hare together, leaving the base open.
Insert the lining and sew on the knitted base.
Sew pompom to back seam for tail.

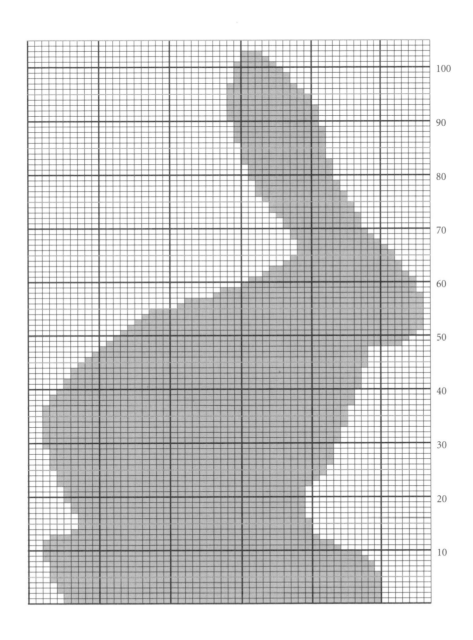

100

90

80

70

60

50

40

30

20

10

SACHET COVER

see pages 28–31

Hang this small scented sachet on the nursery door handle to prevent it from banging and waking up baby. Knitted in crisp mercerized cotton, the gingham design is worked in three colors, then backed with natural linen, trimmed with a picot edge, and finished with a mother-of-pearl button or a dried rosebud. You can fill the sachet with the soothing scent of either dried lavender or rose. An ideal gift for mother or baby.

SIZE
Approximately 5½in/14cm square, including edging

MATERIALS
Small amounts of Yeoman's Cotton Cannele 4-Ply (or a similar super-fine-weight mercerized cotton yarn) in cream (A), light green (B), and dark green (C)
Pair of size 2 (2.75mm) knitting needles
Size B-1 (2mm) crochet hook
6in/14.5cm by 10in/25cm piece of natural linen fabric
18in/45cm of ⅝in/1.5cm wide cotton tape
Mother-of-pearl button or a dried rosebud
Organza fabric approximately 6in/13.5cm by 11in/27cm
Dried lavender or rosebuds to fill sachet

GAUGE
34 sts and 34 rows to 4in/10cm square over pattern using size 2 (2.75mm) needles. Always work a gauge swatch and change needle size if necessary.

ABBREVIATIONS
See page 139.

GINGHAM PATTERN
Worked over a multiple of 8 sts using A and B.
Row 1 (RS) K3A, [2B, 2A] to last st, 1A.
Row 2 P3A, [2B, 2A] to last st, 1A.
Row 3 K3B, [2C, 2B] to last st, 1B.
Row 4 P3B, [2C, 2B] to last st, 1B.
These 4 rows are repeated to form pattern.

SACHET COVER FRONT
With size 2 (2.75mm) needles and A, cast on 48 sts.
Work 5in/12.5 cm in gingham pattern (see above), ending with RS facing for bind-off.
Bind off.

TO FINISH
Weave in any yarn ends.
Lay work out flat and gently steam.

PICOT EDGING
With size B-1 (2mm) crochet hook and A and with RS facing, beg in the center of one edge of knitted front and join yarn with a sl st to a st or row end, then ch 1, 1 sc in same place as sl st, *ch 3, 1 sl st in 3rd ch from hook (1 picot made), skip next st or row end, 1 sc in next st or row end; rep from * along each side, working 2 picot into each corner, join with a sl st to first sc worked.
Fasten off.

SACHET COVER BACK
Cut a piece of natural linen, 6in/14.5cm by 3½in/8cm, for upper back and another, 6in/14.5cm by 5in/13cm, for lower back.
On one 6in/14.5cm edge of each piece, fold under and press ¼in/5mm then ½in/1cm and topstitch this

double hem in place.

Fold under and press ½in/1cm on remaining three sides of each piece.

For the hanging loop, fold cotton tape in half and pin to the center of the wrong side of top edge of knitted front.

With wrong sides together, lay larger back piece (the lower back piece) on knitted square and slipstitch in place around the edge. Lay smaller back piece (the upper back piece) on wrong side of knitted square overlapping the larger back piece and slipstitch in place around the edge, securing the hanging loop in the seam.

Sew a button or a dried rosebud to the center of the knitted front.

FABRIC SACHET BAG

Fold organza fabric in half widthwise and taking a ½in/1cm seam, stitch around two open edges and 1¼in/3cm of the third edge. Turn right-side out, fill with dried lavender or rosebuds, and slipstitch the opening closed.

Insert fabric sachet bag into sachet cover.

RABBIT RATTLE

see pages 32–33

Designed to slip over baby's wrist, this soft rattle is decorated with a cute bunny's head, which contains a bell. It is knitted in exquisite organic cotton yarn, with only the simplest embroidery and ribbon bow details—a perfect project to use up any scraps of left-over yarn.

SIZE
Approximately 3¼in/8cm in diameter

MATERIALS
1 x 1¾oz/50g ball (131yd/120m per ball) of Rowan Purelife Organic Cotton DK Naturally Dyed (or a similar double-knitting-weight organic cotton yarn) in ecru
Pair each of sizes 3 and 6 (3mm and 4mm) knitting needles
Small amount of natural organic cotton stuffing
Small bell
Scraps of contrasting yarn for embroidery
10in/25cm of ⅝in/1.5cm wide ribbon

GAUGE
25 sts and 35 rows to 4in/10cm square over St st using size 3 (3mm) needles. Always work a gauge swatch and change needle size if necessary.

ABBREVIATIONS
See page 139.

RATTLE RING
With size 6 (4mm) needles, cast on 26 sts.
Change to size 3 (3mm) needles and work as follows:

Row 1 (RS) [K1, k into front and back of next st—called kfb] to end of row. **39 sts.**
Beg with a p row, work 3 rows in St st.
Row 5 [K2, kfb] to end of row. **52 sts.**
Beg with a p row, work 13 rows in St st.
Row 19 [K2, k2tog] to end of row. **39 sts.**
Beg with a p row, work 3 rows in St st.
Row 23 [K1, k2tog] to end of row. **26 sts.**
Bind off using size 6 (4mm) needles.

HEAD
With size 3 (3mm) needles, cast on 16 sts.
Row 1 P.
Row 2 [K1, kfb] to end. **24 sts.**
Beg with a p row, work 12 rows in St st.
Row 15 [P2tog] to end of row. **12 sts.**
Cut yarn, thread through rem sts, pull up tightly, and secure firmly.

EARS (MAKE 2)
With size 3 (3mm) needles, cast on 11 sts.
Beg with a k row, work 2 rows in St st.
Cont in St st, dec 1 st at each end of next row and 3 foll RS rows.
Next row P3tog and fasten off.

TO FINISH
Sew together row ends of ring piece, using mattress stitch. Graft the cast-on and bound-off edges together, pushing stuffing into the rattle as you proceed.
Sew head seam, leaving cast-on edge open. Stuff firmly with bell inserted in the center. Run a thread around cast-on edge, pull up tightly, and secure.
Sew ears to head and sew head to rattle.
Embroider face with a cross-stitch and two French knots as shown. Tie ribbon around neck and trim.

HAT AND BOOTS

see pages 34–35

The perfect hat and boots set for top-to-toe style. A simple pull-on hat worked in stripes of green and ecru with rolled brim is complemented by the plain and easy boots knitted in stockinette stitch with contrasting ribbed cuffs and pull-on tabs.

SIZE
To fit 0–3 (3–6: 6–9) months
Length of boot 3¼ (3½: 4)in/8 (9: 10)cm

MATERIALS
2 x 1¾oz/50g balls (131yd/120m per ball) of Rowan Purelife Organic Cotton DK Naturally Dyed (or a similar double-knitting-weight organic cotton yarn) in green (A) and 1 x 1¾oz/50g ball in ecru (B)
Pair each of sizes 3 and 5 (3.25mm and 3.75mm) knitting needles
8in/20cm of ½in/1cm wide cotton tape

GAUGE
22 sts and 30 rows to 4in/10cm square over St st using size 5 (3.75mm) needles. Always work a gauge swatch and change needle size if necessary.

ABBREVIATIONS
See page 139.

HAT

STRIPE COLOR SEQUENCE
11 rows A.
1 row B.
7 rows A.
3 rows B.
5 rows A.
5 rows B.
3 rows A.
10 rows B.
2 rows A.
8 rows B.
2 rows A.
5 rows B.

TO MAKE HAT
With size 3 (3.25mm) needles and A, cast on 73 (82: 91) sts.
Beg with a k row and following the stripe color sequence in St st throughout, work 6 rows in St st. Change to size 5 (3.75mm) needles.
Cont in stripe pattern as set until work measures 5½ (6: 6¼)in/14 (15: 16)cm from cast-on edge, ending with RS facing for next row.
SHAPE TOP
Row 1 (RS) [K7, k2tog] to last st, k1. 65 (73: 81) sts.
Row 2 P.
Row 3 [K6, k2tog] to last st, k1. 57 (64: 71) sts.
Row 4 P.
Row 5 [K5, k2tog] to last st, k1. 49 (55: 61) sts.
Row 6 P.
Row 7 [K4, k2tog] to last st, k1. 41 (46: 51) sts.
Row 8 P.
Row 9 [K3, k2tog] to last st, k1. 33 (37: 41) sts.
Row 10 P.

Row 11 [K2, k2tog] to last st, k1. 25 (28: 31) sts.
Row 12 P.
Row 13 [K1, k2tog] to last st, k1. 17 (19: 21) sts.
Row 14 [K2tog] to last st, k1. 9 (10: 11) sts.
Cut yarn leaving a long end and thread through rem sts. Pull up tightly and secure firmly. Leave long yarn end to use for seam.

TO FINISH
Sew seam, reversing seam at lower edge to allow brim to roll.
Weave in any yarn ends. Gently steam.

BOOTS

TO MAKE BOOTS (MAKE TWO)
The boot is made in one piece starting at the sole.
SOLE
With size 3 (3.25mm) needles and A, cast on 32 (38: 44) sts.
Beg with a k row work in St st, shaping as follows:
Row 1 (RS) [K2, m1, k13 (16: 19), m1] twice, k2. 36 (42: 48) sts.
Row 2 P.
Row 3 [K2, m1, k15 (18: 21), m1] twice, k2. 40 (46: 52) sts.
Row 4 P.
Row 5 [K2, m1, k17 (20: 23), m1] twice, k2. 44 (50: 56) sts.
Row 6 P.
Row 7 (RS) P (to form ridge on RS dividing sole from upper).
UPPER
Beg with a p row, work 5 (7: 7) rows in St st, so ending with RS facing for next row.

SHAPE FOOT
Row 1 (RS) K20 (23: 26) sts, k2tog tbl, k2tog, k to end. 42 (48: 54) sts.
Row 2 P19 (22: 25) sts, p2tog, p2tog tbl, p to end. 40 (46: 52) sts.
Row 3 K18 (21: 24) sts, k2tog tbl, k2tog, k to end. 38 (44: 50) sts.
Row 4 P17 (20: 23) sts, p2tog, p2tog tbl, p to end. 36 (42: 48) sts.
Row 5 K16 (19: 22) sts, k2tog tbl, k2tog, k to end. 34 (40: 46) sts.
Row 6 P15 (18: 21) sts, p2tog, p2tog tbl, p to end. 32 (38: 44) sts.
Row 7 K14 (17: 20) sts, k2tog tbl, k2tog, k to end. 30 (36: 42) sts.
Row 8 P.
Row 9 K13 (16: 19) sts, k2tog tbl, k2tog, k to end. 28 (34: 40) sts.
Row 10 P.
Row 11 [K1, p1] to end of row.
Rep last row 13 (17: 22) times more.
Bind off loosely but evenly in rib.
Make second boot in exactly same way.

TO FINISH
Fold cast-on edge in half and sew seam to form sole.
Sew back seam from sole to top of ankle cuff.
Fold rib in half to wrong side and slipstitch in place.
Cut tape in half, then fold each piece in half to form a loop. Sew one loop to the inside back seam at lower edge of ribbing on each boot.

FAIR ISLE BUNTING

see pages 38–39

A simple and stylish project to make for a new baby, this bunting is knitted in stockinette stitch, finished with a ribbed edge, and topped off with a fluffy pompom. It makes a practical and snug "bag" for baby. The Fair Isle pattern is worked in only two colors, but the bunting would be just as effective knitted in a single color with a contrasting ribbing.

SIZE
Length approximately 27½in/70cm to top of hood

MATERIALS
6 x 1¾oz/50g balls (131yd/120m per ball) of Rowan Purelife Organic Cotton DK Naturally Dyed (or a similar double-knitting-weight organic cotton yarn) in pink (A) and 2 x 1¾oz/50g balls in gray (B)
Pair of size 5 (3.75mm) knitting needles
One size 3 (3.25mm) circular knitting needle

GAUGE
22 sts and 30 rows to 4in/10cm square over St st pattern using size 5 (3.75mm) needles. Always work a gauge swatch and change needle size if necessary.

ABBREVIATIONS
See page 139.

TIPS AND TECHNIQUES
* The chart is worked over 90 sts and 60 rows, which are repeated.
* Strand yarn not in use across WS of work, weaving it in every 2 to 3 stitches.
* Use a separate ball of yarn for each motif on chart rows 13–21, twisting yarn at color change to avoid holes.

BACK
With size 5 (3.75mm) needles and A, cast on 90 sts.
Beg with a k row, work 210 rows in St st from chart, so ending with row 30 of 4th repeat.
Bind off.

FRONT
With size 5 (3.75mm) needles and A, cast on 90 sts.
Beg with a k row, work 150 rows in St st from chart, so ending with row 30 of 3rd repeat.
Bind off.

TO FINISH
Lay pieces out flat and gently steam.
Fold cast-on edge of back in half and sew seam to form top edge of hood. Matching pattern, sew side seams from bound-off edges of back and front up to cast-on edge of front. Sew bound-off edges of front to back to form lower edge of bunting.
EDGING
With size 3 (3.25mm) circular needle and B and with RS facing, pick up and k 90 sts across cast-on edge of front, 57 sts up row ends of back to hood seam and 57 sts down row ends of back to cast-on edge of front. **204 sts.**
Working in rows not rounds, work 5 rows in k1, p1 rib.
Bind off in rib.
Sew edging seam.
Weave in any yarn ends.
With B, make a 2¼in/6cm pompom (see page 90) and sew to point of hood.

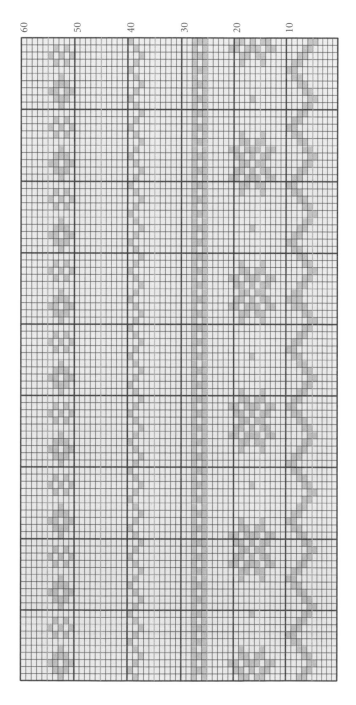

A pink

B gray

FIRST BLANKET

see pages 40–41

This elegant blanket is the ideal gift to welcome a new baby into the world. Made in exquisite natural bamboo yarn, the main basic garter stitch is complemented by a simple decorative edging. Tie the folded blanket with a sumptuous cotton velvet bow and then wrap in tissue paper for a memorable gift.

SIZE
Approximately 33½in/85cm x 41¾in/106cm, including edging

MATERIALS
15 x 1¾oz/50g balls (112yd/102m per ball) of Rowan Classic (RYC) Bamboo Soft (or a similar double-knitting-weight bamboo yarn) in silver-gray
Pair of size 5 (3.75mm) knitting needles

GAUGE
22 sts and 42 rows to 4in/10cm square over garter st using size 5 (3.75mm) needles. Always work a gauge swatch and change needle size if necessary.

ABBREVIATIONS
See page 139.

MAIN PIECE
Cast on 175 sts.
Work 39¼in/100cm in garter st (k every row).
Bind off.

EDGING
Cast on 5 sts.
Row 1 (RS) K.
Row 2 K2, m1, k3. 6 sts.
Row 3 K4, m1, k2. 7 sts.
Row 4 K3, m1, k4. 8 sts.
Row 5 K5, m1, k3. 9 sts.
Row 6 Bind off 4 sts, k to end. 5 sts.
Rep last 6 rows until work measures approximately 143¾in/365cm, ending with a patt row 5.
Bind off all sts.

TO FINISH
Weave in any yarn ends.
Slipstitch edging to main piece, gently gathering edging around corners.

DRESS AND PANTIES

see pages 42–45

A fine milk cotton yarn is used to make this basic little dress and panties set. The dress is knitted in plain stockinette stitch, with picot-edge details on the cuffs and hem, and has a practical and neat open back that ties with linen tapes. The panties are worked in simple garter stitch with a linen tape that ties at the waist.

SIZES
To fit 0–3 (3–6: 6–9) months
DRESS
Knitted chest measurement 19 (20: 21½)in/48 (51: 55)cm
Length to shoulder 12 (13: 14)in/30.5 (33: 35.5)cm
Sleeve length 5¾ (6: 6½)in/14.5 (15.5: 16.5)cm

MATERIALS
DRESS
4 (4: 5) x 1¾oz/50g balls (164yd/150 per ball) of Rowan Fine Milk Cotton (or a similar super-fine-weight cotton-blend yarn) in beige
PANTS
2 x 1¾oz/50g balls (164yd/150 per ball) of Rowan Fine Milk Cotton (or a similar super-fine-weight cotton-blend yarn) in beige
BOTH DRESS AND PANTS
Pair each of sizes 1 and 2 (2.25mm and 2.75mm) knitting needles
79in/2m of ⅝in/1.5cm wide linen tape

GAUGES
27 sts and 54 rows to 4in/10cm square over garter st using size 2 (2.75mm) needles.

29 sts and 38 rows to 4in/10cm square over St st using size 2 (2.75mm) needles.
Always work a gauge swatch and change needle size if necessary.

ABBREVIATIONS
See page 139.

TIPS AND TECHNIQUES
* The garter stitch panties are worked in one piece from the front waistband, with the back waist shaped with short rows.

DRESS

FRONT
With size 2 (2.75mm) needles, cast on 102 (108: 114) sts.
Beg with a k row, work 4 rows in St st.
Next row (picot hem) (RS) K1, [yo, k2tog] to last st, k1.
Beg with a p row, cont in St st until work measures 8½ (8¾: 9¼)in/21.5 (22.5: 23.5)cm from cast-on edge, ending with RS facing for next row.
FRONT YOKE
Next row (RS) K5, [k2tog, k1] to last 7 sts, k2tog, k5. 71 (75: 79) sts.
K 3 rows.
SHAPE ARMHOLES
Beg with a k row, work in St st throughout as follows:
Bind off 4 sts at beg of next 2 rows. 63 (67: 71) sts.
Dec 1 st at each end of next row and every foll alt row until 51 (55: 59) sts rem.
Work even until armhole measures 2¼ (3: 3½)in/ 6 (7.5: 9)cm, ending with RS facing for next row.

DIVIDE FOR NECK

Next row (RS) K21 (22: 23) sts, turn and leave rem sts on a holder.

P 1 row.

Dec 1 st at neck edge on next row and every foll row until 15 (16: 17) sts rem.

Work even until armhole measures 4 (4½: 5)in/ 10 (11.5: 13)cm, ending with RS facing for next row.

SHAPE SHOULDER

Bind off 5 sts at beg of next row and foll alt row. 5 (6: 7) sts.

Work 1 row.

Bind off rem sts.

With RS facing, slip center 9 (11: 13) sts onto a holder, rejoin yarn to rem sts, k to end of row and complete to match first side of neck, reversing shaping.

LEFT BACK

With size 2 (2.75mm) needles, cast on 54 (57: 60) sts and work as follows:

Row 1 (RS) [K1, p1] 3 times, k to end of row.

Row 2 P to last 6 sts, [k1, p1] 3 times.

Rep last 2 rows once more.

Next row (picot hem) (RS) K1, [yo, k2tog] to last 1 (0: 1) st, k1 (0: 1).

Next row Rep row 2.

Next row Rep row 1.

Next row Rep row 2.

Rep last 2 rows until work measures 8½ (8¾: 9¼)in/ 21.5 (22.5: 23.5)cm from cast-on edge, ending RS facing for next row.

BACK YOKE

Next row (RS) [K1, p1] 3 times, k13 (16: 19) sts, [k2tog] 15 times, k5. 39 (42: 45) sts.

Work 4 rows in garter stitch with 6-st rib border as set, ending with WS facing for next row.

SHAPE ARMHOLE

Next row (WS) Bind off 4 sts, p to last 6 sts, [k1, p1] 3 times. 35 (38: 41) sts.

Cont to work in St st with rib border, and shape as follows:

Dec 1 st at armhole edge on next row and every foll alt row until 29 (32: 35) sts rem.

Work even until armhole measures 4 (4½: 5)in/10 (11.5: 13)cm, ending at armhole edge.

SHAPE SHOULDER AND BACK NECK

Bind off 5 sts at beg of next row. 24 (27: 30) sts.

Work 1 row.

Next row Bind off 5 sts, work until there are 8 (9: 10) sts on right-hand needle, turn and leave rem 11 (13: 15) sts on a holder.

Bind off 3 sts at beg of next row.

Bind off rem 5 (6: 7) sts.

RIGHT BACK

With size 2 (2.75mm) needles, cast on 54 (57: 60) sts and work as follows:

Row 1 (RS) K to last 6 sts, [p1, k1] 3 times.

Row 2 [P1, k1] 3 times, p to end.

Rep last 2 rows once more.

Next row (picot hem) (RS) K1, [yo, k2tog] to last 1 (0: 1) st, k1 (0: 1).

Next row Rep row 2.

Next row Rep row 1.

Next row Rep row 2.

Rep last 2 rows until work measures 8½ (8¾: 9¼)in/ 21.5 (22.5: 23.5)cm from cast-on edge, ending with RS facing for next row.

FRONT YOKE

Next row (RS) K5, [k2tog] 15 times, k13 (16: 19) sts, [p1, k1] 3 times. 39 (42: 45) sts.

Work 3 rows in garter stitch with 6-st rib border as

set, ending with RS facing for next row.

Next row (RS) Bind off 4 sts, k to last 6 sts, [p1, k1] 3 times. 35 (38: 41) sts.

Cont to work in St st with rib border, work 1 row, then shape as follows:

Dec 1 st at armhole edge on next row and every foll alt row until 29 (32: 35) sts rem.

Work even until armhole measures 4 (4½: 5)in/10 (11.5: 13)cm, ending at armhole edge.

SHAPE SHOULDER AND BACK NECK

Bind off 5 sts at beg of next row. 24 (27: 30) sts.
Work 1 row.

Next row Bind off 5 sts, work until there are 8 (9: 10) sts on right-hand needle, turn and leave rem 11 (13: 15) sts on a holder.

Bind off 3 sts at beg of next row.
Bind off rem 5 (6: 7) sts.

SLEEVES

With size 2 (2.75mm) needles, cast on 38 (42: 46) sts and beg with a k row, work 4 rows in St st.

Next row (picot hem) (RS) K1, [yo, k2tog] to last st, k1.

Beg with a p row, cont in St st and inc 1 st at each end of 4th row and every foll 6th row until there are 56 (60: 64) sts.

Work even until sleeve measures 5¾ (6: 6½)in/ 14.5 (15.5: 16.5)cm from picot row, ending with RS facing for next row.

SHAPE TOP OF SLEEVE

Bind off 4 sts at beg of next 2 rows. 48 (52: 56) sts.
Work even for 2 rows.

Dec 1 st at each end of next row and foll 4th row, then every foll alt row until 30 (34: 38) sts rem, ending with WS facing for next row.

Next row (WS) P7, [p2tog] 8 (10: 12) times, p7. 22 (24: 26) sts.
Bind off.

NECKBAND

Sew both shoulder seams.

With size 1 (2.25mm) needles and RS facing, rejoin yarn and rib as set across first 6 sts from left back holder and k rem 5 (7: 9) sts, then pick up and k 3 sts from left back neck edge, 14 sts down left front neck, k 9 (11: 13) sts from center front holder, pick up and k 14 sts up right front neck, 3 sts along right back neck edge, k first 5 (7: 9) sts from right back holder, then rib rem 6 sts from holder as set. 65 (71: 77) sts.

Work 3 rows in k1, p1 rib as set.
Bind off in rib.

TO FINISH

Weave in any yarn ends.
Gently steam work.
Sew sleeves into armholes, easing to fit.
Sew side and sleeve seams.
Turn hems to wrong side along picot edge and slipstitch in place.
Cut four lengths of linen tape each 23cm long and sew in pairs to either side of back opening, one pair just at start of neckband and the other pair at lower edge of yoke.

PANTIES

TO MAKE PANTIES

With size 2 (2.75mm) needles, cast on 52 (56: 60) sts and work in rib as follows:

Row 1 (RS) K2, [p1, k1] to last 2 sts, p2.

Rows 2, 3, and 4 Rep row 1.

Row 5 (eyelet row) K2, [yo, k2tog, p1, k1] to last 2 sts, yo, k2tog.

Rows 6, 7, 8, and 9 Rep row 1.

Next row (inc row) K6 (6: 7), [k into front and back of next st, k12 (13: 14)] 3 times, k into front and back of next st, k6 (7: 7). **56 (60: 64) sts.**

Cont in garter st (k every row) throughout, work even for 53 (63: 73) rows.

DIVIDE FOR LEGS

Row 1 K18 (19: 20) sts, turn and leave rem sts on a spare needle.

Row 2 K1, k2tog, k15 (16: 17).

Row 3 K14 (15: 16) sts, k2tog, k1.

Row 4 K1, k2tog, k13 (14: 15) sts.

Cont to dec in this way until 2 sts rem.

Next row K2tog and fasten off.

With RS facing, rejoin yarn and k across 38 (41: 44) sts on spare needle, then work as follows:

Row 1 K15 (16: 17), k2tog, k1, turn and leave rem sts on a spare needle.

Row 2 K1, k2tog, k14 (15: 16) sts.

Row 3 K13 (14: 15) sts, k2tog, k1.

Row 4 K1, k2tog, k12 (13: 14) sts.

Cont to decrease in this way until 2 sts rem.

Next row K2tog and fasten off.

With RS facing, rejoin yarn to rem 20 (22: 24) sts.

Cont in garter st throughout, work even in garter st for 9 (13: 17) rows.

Inc 1 st at each end of next row and every foll alt row until there are 56 (60: 64) sts.

Work even for 71 (81: 93) rows.

SHAPE BACK

Rows 1 and 2 K to last 3 sts, turn.

Rows 3 and 4 K to last 6 sts, turn.

Rows 5 and 6 K to last 9 sts, turn.

Rows 7 and 8 K to last 12 sts, turn.

Rows 9 and 10 K to last 15 sts, turn.

Rows 11 and 12 K to last 18 sts, turn.

Rows 13 and 14 K across all sts.

Row 15 K6 (6: 7) [k2tog, k12 (13: 14)] 3 times, k2tog, k6 (7: 7). **52 (56: 60) sts.**

Row 16 K2, [p1, k1] to last 2 sts, p2.

Rep last row 3 times more.

Next row (eyelet row) K2, [yo, k2tog, p1, k1] to last 2 sts, yo, k2tog.

Next row K2, [p1, k1] to last 2 sts, p2.

Rep last row 3 times more.

Bind off in rib.

TO FINISH

Sew side seams.

Cut approximately 32in/80cm of linen tape, thread through the eyelets and tie in a bow at the front.

RECYCLED-RAG BASKET

see pages 46–47

Fabric from favorite discarded or worn clothes, or bargain remnants, are washed and cut into strips of "yarn" for this basket. The basket is knitted in seed stitch into a basic cross-shape that assembles into a simple box shape. Make both sizes for the nursery to keep essential creams and lotions at hand, or to store other little odds and ends.

SIZES
Small basket 6¼in/16cm wide x 6¼in/16cm long x 6¼in/16cm tall
Large basket 8in/20cm wide x 11½in/29cm long x 4¾in/12cm tall

MATERIALS
Lengths of linens in various colors—approximately ½yd/50cm cut into ⅝in/1.5cm wide strips and rolled into balls—these baskets were made from a mixture of natural linens, pale and dark lavender linen, brown gingham linen, and a dishtowel stripe
Pair of size 10½ (6.5mm) knitting needles
Large-eyed blunt-ended sewing needle

TIPS AND TECHNIQUES
* Instructions for the large basket are given in parentheses.
* When changing to another fabric, hold two ends together and work the next stitch, rather than knotting the two ends, which can look lumpy.
* Weave any long ends into the fabric when you have finished knitting.

TO MAKE SMALL (LARGE) BASKET
Cast on 11 (15) sts.
Row 1 K1, [p1, k1] to end.
Last row is repeated to form seed st.
Work 6¼ (4¾)in/16 (12)cm in seed st as set.
Keeping seed st correct as set throughout, cast on 12 (9) sts at beg of next 2 rows. 35 (33) sts.
Work even in seed st for 6¼ (11½)in/16(29)cm more.
Bind off 12 (9) sts at the beg of the next 2 rows. 11 (15) sts.
Work even in seed st for 6¼ (4¾)in/16 (12)cm more on rem sts.
Bind off in seed st.

TO FINISH
Weave in any "yarn" ends.
Lay work out flat and fold each corner up in turn.
Overcast stitch each corner together in turn with a strip of fabric.
For added rigidity, if required, overcast stitch all around top edge.

SWEATER AND PANTS

see pages 48–49

These basic pieces, knitted in organic cotton for ultimate comfort, pair a simple sweater with easy pull-on pants with roll-edge cuffs and a back pocket.

SIZES
To fit 0–3 (3–6: 6–9) months
SWEATER
Knitted chest measurement 22 (23: 25)in/54 (58: 62)cm
Length from shoulder 9¾ (10¾: 12)in/24.5 (27.5: 30.5)cm
Sleeve length 5¾ (6½: 7¾)in/14.5 (16.5: 19.5)cm

MATERIALS
SWEATER
3 (4: 4) x 1¾oz/50g balls (131yd/120m per ball) of Rowan Purelife Organic Cotton DK Naturally Dyed (or a similar double-knitting-weight organic cotton yarn) in blue
2 horn buttons ⅝in/1.5cm in diameter
PANTS
3 (3: 4) x 1¾oz/50g balls (131yd/120m per ball) of Rowan Purelife Organic Cotton DK Naturally Dyed (or a similar double-knitting-weight organic cotton yarn) in green
Waist length of ¾in/2cm wide elastic
BOTH SWEATER AND PANTS
Pair each of sizes 3 and 5 (3.25mm and 3.75mm) knitting needles

GAUGE
22 sts and 30 rows to 4in/10cm square over St st using size 5 (3.75mm) needles. Always work a gauge swatch and change needle size if necessary.

ABBREVIATIONS
See page 139.

TIPS AND TECHNIQUES
* Work fully fashioned increases as follows:
K3, m1, k to last 3 sts, m1, k3.
* Work fully fashioned decreases as follows:
K3, k2tog, k to last 5 sts, k2tog tbl, k3.

SWEATER

BACK
With size 3 (3.25mm) needles, cast on 60 (64: 68) sts and beg with a k row, work 6 rows in St st.
Change to size 5 (3.75mm) needles and cont in St st until Back measures 5¾ (6: 7¼)in/14.5 (16.5: 18.5)cm from cast-on edge, ending with RS facing for next row.
SHAPE ARMHOLES
Cont in St st throughout, bind off 3 sts at beg of next 2 rows. **54 (58: 62) sts.**
Dec 1 st at each end of next row and 3 foll alt rows (see note on fully fashioned decreases). **46 (50: 54) sts.**
Work even until armholes measure 4 (4¼: 4¾)in/ 10 (11: 12)cm, ending with RS facing for next row.
SHAPE BACK NECK AND SHOULDERS
Next row (RS) K15 (16: 18) sts, turn and leave rem sts on a spare needle.
Next row Bind off 2 sts, p to end of row.
Work even for 2 rows.
Bind off rem 13 (14: 16) sts.
Return to rem sts on spare needle and with RS facing, slip center 16 (18: 18) sts onto a holder, rejoin yarn to rem sts and k to end of row.
Next row P.
Next row Bind off 2 sts, k to end of row. **13 (14: 16) sts.**

Next row P.
Change to size 3 (3.25mm) needles.
Next row [K1, p1] to last 1 (0: 0) st, k1 (0: 0).
Next row P1 (0: 0), [k1, p1] to end.
Rep last 2 rows twice more. Bind off in rib.

FRONT
Work as for Back until armhole measures 2¾ (3: 3½)in/7 (8: 9)cm, ending with RS facing for next row.
SHAPE NECK
Next row (RS) K19 (20: 22) sts, turn and leave rem sts on a spare needle.
Next row Bind off 3 sts, p to end of row.
Work even for 1 row.
Dec 1 st at neck edge on every row until 13 (14: 16) sts rem.
Work even until armhole measures 4 (4¼: 4¾)in/ 10 (11: 12)cm, ending with RS facing for next row.
Change to size 3 (3.25mm) needles.
Next row (RS) [K1, p1] to last 1 (0: 0) st, k1 (0: 0).
Next row P1 (0: 0), [k1, p1] to end.
Next row (buttonhole row) Rib 3, yo, k2tog, rib 3 (4: 6) sts, yo, work 2tog, rib 3.
Work 3 rows more in rib. Bind off in rib.
Return to rem sts on spare needle and with RS facing, slip 8 (10: 10) sts at center front onto a holder, rejoin yarn to rem sts, bind off 3 sts, k to end.
P 1 row.
Dec 1 st at neck edge on every row until 13 (14: 16) sts rem.
Work even in St st until armhole measures 4¼ (4¾: 5)in/11 (12: 13)cm. Bind off.

SLEEVES
With size 3 (3.25mm) needles, cast on 38 (40: 42) sts and beg with a k row, work 6 rows in St st.

Change to size 5 (3.75mm) needles.
Cont in St st, inc 1 st at each end of 3rd row and every foll 6th row until there are 50 (54: 58) sts.
Work even until sleeve measures 5¾ (6½: 7¾)in/ 14.5 (16.5: 19.5)cm from cast-on edge, ending with RS facing for next row.
SHAPE TOP OF SLEEVE
Bind off 3 sts at beg of next 4 (4: 6) rows. 38 (42: 40) sts.
Bind off 2 sts at beg of next 4 (6: 2) rows. 30 (30: 36) sts.
Bind off 3 sts at beg of next 4 (2: 4) rows. 18 (24: 24) sts.
Bind off 4 sts at beg of next 2 rows. 10 (16: 16) sts.
Bind off.

NECKBAND
Sew right shoulder seam.
With size 3 (3.25mm) needles and RS facing, pick up and k 13 (14: 16) sts along rib and down left front neck, k across 8 (10: 10) sts from center front holder, pick up and k 13 (14: 16) sts up right front neck, 3 sts down right back neck, k across 16 (18: 18) sts from center back holder, then pick up and k 8 sts from left back neck and along rib. 61 (65: 71) sts.
Beg with a p row, work 7 rows in St st.
Bind off.

POCKET (MAKE ONE)
With size 5 (3.75mm) needles, cast on 8 (10: 12) sts and beg with a k row, work 2 rows in St st.
Cont in St st throughout, inc 1 st at each end of next row and 2 foll alt rows. 14 (16: 18) sts.
Work even until pocket measures 2¼ (2¾: 3¼)in/ 6 (7: 8)cm, ending with WS facing for next row.
Change to size 3 (3.25mm) needles and work 2 rows in St st.
Bind off purlwise.

TO FINISH
Weave in any yarn ends. Gently steam work.
Place buttonhole band over button band and
slipstitch edges together along armhole edge.
Sew sleeves into armholes, easing to fit.
Sew side and sleeve seams. Sew on buttons.
Sew on pocket 4 (4¼: 4¾)in/10 (11: 12)cm down
from shoulder and 2in/5cm in from side seam.

PANTS

RIGHT LEG
With size 5 (3.75mm) needles, cast on 52 (54: 56) sts
and beg with a k row, work 7 rows in St st, ending
with WS facing for next row.
Next row (WS) K (to form fold-line ridge on RS).
Beg with a k row, work 8 rows in St st.
SHAPE BACK
Row 1 K10 (11: 12) sts, turn.
Row 2 P to end.
Row 3 K21 (22: 23) sts, turn.
Row 4 P to end.
Row 5 K32 (33: 34) sts, turn.
Row 6 P to end.
Row 7 K43 (44: 45) sts, turn.
Row 8 P to end.
Work even in St st across all 52 (54: 56) sts for 16
(18: 22) rows more.
**Inc 1 st (see note on fully fashioned increases) at
each end of next row and every foll 6th row until
there are 62 (64: 66) sts.
Work even for 3 rows.
Cast on 4 sts at beg of next 2 rows. 70 (72: 74) sts.
SHAPE LEG
Dec 1 st (see note on fully fashioned decreases) at

each end of 5th row and every foll 6th row until
60 (62: 64) sts rem.
Work even for 3 (9: 15) rows, ending with RS facing
for next row.
Change to size 3 (3.25mm) needles and work 6 rows
in St st. Bind off.**

LEFT LEG
With size 5 (3.75mm) needles, cast on 52 (54: 56) sts
and beg with a k row, work 7 rows in St st, ending
with WS facing for next row.
Next row (WS) K (to form fold-line ridge on RS).
Beg with a k row, work 9 rows in St st.
SHAPE BACK
Row 1 P10 (11: 12) sts, turn.
Row 2 K to end.
Row 3 P21 (22: 23) sts, turn.
Row 4 K to end.
Row 5 P32 (33: 34) sts, turn.
Row 6 K to end.
Row 7 P43 (44: 45) sts, turn.
Row 8 K to end.
Work even in St st across all 52 (54: 56) sts for 15
(17: 21) rows more.
Complete as for Right Leg from ** to **.

POCKET (MAKE ONE)
Work exactly as for Sweater pocket.

TO FINISH
Weave in any yarn ends. Lay work out flat and gently
steam. Sew back and front seams. Sew leg seam,
reversing seam at lower edge, to allow hems to roll.
Turn waistband to inside along ridge row and
slipstitch in place, leaving a gap. Insert elastic, sew
ends together, and sew up gap in seam. Sew on pocket.

BOOTIES AND BONNET

see pages 52–55

K nitted in a lacy pattern, these pretty, dainty shoes have garter stitch soles and uppers and are fastened with a tiny natural mother-of-pearl button. The hat is a simple pull-on design worked in garter stitch and edged with a shell edging. The set is made in fine milk cotton yarn.

SIZES
To fit 0–3 (3–6: 6–9) months
Length of booties 3¼ (3½: 4)in/8 (9: 10)cm

MATERIALS
1 x 1¾oz/50g ball (164yd/150m per ball) of Rowan Fine Milk Cotton (or a similar super-fine-weight cotton-blend yarn) in pink or white
Pair of size 2 (2.75mm) knitting needles
2 small mother-of-pearl buttons for shoes
1 mother-of-pearl button for hat flower

GAUGE
30 sts and 38 rows to 4in/10cm square over St st using size 2 (2.75mm) needles. Always work a gauge swatch and change needle size if necessary.

ABBREVIATIONS
See page 139.

BOOTIES

LEFT UPPER
Using two strands of yarn held together, cast on 50 (58: 66) sts.
Cut one strand of yarn and cont with a single strand of yarn, k 3 rows.
Next row K1, *p1, yo, k1; rep from * to last st, k1. 74 (86: 98) sts.
Next row K1, *p1, yo, k2tog; rep from * to last st, k1.
Rep last row 2 (4: 4) times more.
Next row K2, *p1, k2tog; rep from * to end of row. 50 (58: 66) sts.
Cont in garter st (k every row) as follows:
Next row K20 (24: 28), k2tog, k6, k2tog, k20 (24: 28). 48 (56: 64) sts.
Next row K19 (23: 27), k2tog, k6, k2tog, k19 (23: 27). 46 (54: 62) sts.
Next row K18 (22: 26), k2tog, k6, k2tog, k18 (22: 26). 44 (52: 60) sts.
Next row K17 (21: 25), k2tog, k6, k2tog, k17 (21: 25). 42 (50: 58) sts.
Next row K16 (20: 24), k2tog, k6, k2tog, k16 (20: 24). 40 (48: 56) sts.
Next row K15 (19: 23), k2tog, k6, k2tog, k15 (19: 23). 38 (46: 54) sts.
Next row K14 (18: 22), k2tog, k6, k2tog, k14 (18: 22). 36 (44: 52) sts.**
Next row K10 (12: 14) sts, turn and leave rem sts on a holder.
K 3 rows.
Bind off.
Rejoin yarn to rem sts, bind off center 16 (20: 24) sts, cast on 12 (14: 16) sts onto left needle and k to end of row. 22 (26: 30) sts.

Next row (buttonhole row) K to last 3 sts, yo, k2tog, k1.
K 2 rows.
Bind off.

RIGHT UPPER
Work as Left Upper to **.
Next row K10 (12: 14) sts, turn and leave rem 26 (32: 38) sts on a spare needle.
Next row Cast on 12 (14: 16) sts onto left needle and k to end of row. 22 (26: 30) sts.
K 1 row.
Next row (buttonhole row) K to last 3 sts, yo, k2tog, k1.
K 2 rows.
Bind off.
Rejoin yarn to rem sts, bind off center 16 (20: 24) sts, k to end of row.
K 3 rows.
Bind off.

SOLES (MAKE TWO)
Using two strands of yarn held together throughout, cast on 8 sts.
K 4 rows.
Cont in garter st (k every row) throughout, inc 1 st at each end of row. 10 sts.
Work 4 (6: 8) rows.
Dec 1 st at each end of next row. 8 sts.
Work 6 (7: 8) rows.
Inc 1 st at each end of next row. 10 sts.
Work 4 (6: 8) rows.
Inc 1 st at each end of next row. 12 sts.
Work 4 rows.
Dec 1 st at each end of next 3 rows. 6 sts.
Bind off.

TO FINISH
Sew heel seam. Sew sole to upper.
Weave in any yarn ends.
Sew on buttons.

BONNET
With size 2 (2.75mm) needles, cast on 97 (112: 127) sts and work as follows:
Row 1 (RS) K1, yo, *k5, slip the 2nd, 3rd, 4th, and 5th sts over the first st, yo; rep from * to last st, k1.
Row 2 P1, *[p1, yo, k1 tbl] all into next st, p1; rep from * to end. 81 (93: 105) sts.
Row 3 K and dec 1 st at end of row. 80 (92: 104) sts.
Rows 4, 5, and 6 K1, *p1, yo, k2tog; rep from * to last st, k1.
Row 7 K and inc 1(dec 1: dec 3) sts evenly across row. 81 (91: 101) sts.
Cont in garter st (k every row) until hat measures 3¼ (4: 4½)in/8.5 (10: 11.5)cm from cast-on edge.
SHAPE TOP
Cont in garter st throughout, shape top as follows:
Next row K1, [k2tog, k8] to end of row. 73 (82: 91) sts.
Work 3 rows.
Next row K1, [k2tog, k7] to end of row. 65 (73: 81) sts.
Work 3 rows.
Next row K1, [k2tog, k6] to end of row. 57 (64: 71) sts.
Work 3 rows.
Next row K1, [k2tog, k5] to end of row. 49 (55: 61) sts.
Work 3 rows.
Next row K1, [k2tog, k4] to end of row. 41 (46: 51) sts.

Work 1 row.
Next row K1, [k2tog, k3] to end of row.
33 (37: 41) sts.
Work 1 row.
Next row K1, [k2tog, k2] to end of row.
25 (28: 31) sts.
Work 1 row.
Next row K1, [k2tog, k1] to end of row.
17 (19: 21) sts.
Next row K1, [k2tog] to end of row. 9 (10: 11) sts.
Cut yarn leaving long end, thread through rem sts,
pull up tightly, and secure firmly.

LACE FLOWER
With size 2 (2.75mm) needles, cast on 49 sts.
Row 1 (WS) P.
Row 2 K1, *yo, k1, sl 1, k2tog, psso, k1, yo, k1; rep
from * to end of row.
Rep last 2 rows twice more.
Next row P.
Next row [P2tog] to last st, p1. 25 sts.
Next row [K2tog] to last st, k1. 13 sts.
Cut yarn, thread through rem sts, pull up tightly, and
secure firmly.

TO FINISH
Sew hat seam.
Sew flower seam.
Weave in any yarn ends.
Sew flower securely to hat, stitching on button
through center of flower and through hat.

LACE PILLOW

see pages 56–57

Pretty yet simple, this pillow cover is knitted in a collection of lace stitch, eyelets, and seed stitch for texture, and the back is worked in basic stockinette stitch. The pillow is finished with a softly gathered lacy edging and natural cotton ties.

SIZE
Approximately 16in/40cm x 12in/30cm

MATERIALS
4 x 1¾oz/50g balls (120yd/110m per ball) of Lanaknits Cashmere Canapa (or a similar double knitting-weight cashmere/cotton-blend yarn) in ecru
Pair of size 5 (3.75mm) knitting needles
Feather pillow form to fit cover
60in/1.5m of ½in/1cm wide cotton tape for ties

GAUGE
22 sts and 34 rows to 4in/10cm square over St st using size 5 (3.75mm) needles. Always work a gauge swatch and change needle size if necessary.

ABBREVIATIONS
See page 139.

TIPS AND TECHNIQUES
* The back of the pillow is worked in stockinette stitch with a single rib border along one side edge.

FRONT
Cast on 87 sts and work in seed st and lace pattern as follows:
Row 1 K1, [p1, k1] 28 times, k5, p2, k9, yo, k1, yo, k3, sl 1, k2tog, psso, p2, k5.
Row 2 and every foll WS row P30, [k1, p1] 28 times, k1.
Row 3 K1, [p1, k1] 28 times, k5, p2, k10, yo, k1, yo, k2, sl 1, k2tog, psso, p2, k5.
Row 5 (eyelet row) K1, [p1, k1] 28 times, k2, yo, k2tog, k1, p2, k3tog, k4, yo, k1, yo, k3, [yo, k1] twice, sl 1, k2tog, psso, p2, k2, yo, k2tog, k1.
Row 7 K1, [p1, k1] 28 times, k5, p2, k3tog, k3, yo, k1, yo, k9, p2, k5.
Row 9 K1, [p1, k1] 28 times, k5, p2, k3tog, k2, yo, k1, yo, k10, p2, k5.
Row 11 (eyelet row) K1, [p1, k1] 28 times, k2, yo, k2tog, k1, p2, k3tog, [k1, yo] twice, k3, yo, k1, yo, k4, sl 1, k2tog, psso, p2, k2, yo, k2tog, k1.
Row 12 P30, [k1, p1] 28 times, k1.
Rep last 12 rows until work measures 12in/30cm from cast-on edge, ending with RS facing for bind-off.
Bind off.

BACK
Cast on 87 sts and work as follows:
Row 1 [K1, p1] 3 times, k to end of row.
Row 2 P to last 6 sts, [k1, p1] 3 times.
Rep last 2 rows until work measures 12in/30cm from cast-on edge, ending with RS facing for bind-off.
Bind off.

DOUBLE DIAMOND LACE EDGING
Cast on 9 sts.
Row 1 and every alternate row (RS) K.
Row 2 K3, k2tog, yo, k2tog, [yo, k1] twice. **10 sts.**

Row 4 K2, [k2tog, yo] twice, k3, yo, k1. 11 sts.
Row 6 K1, [k2tog, yo] twice, k5, yo, k1. 12 sts.
Row 8 K3, [yo, k2tog] twice, k1, k2tog, yo, k2tog.
11 sts.
Row 10 K4, yo, k2tog, yo, k3tog, yo, k2tog. 10 sts.
Row 12 K5, yo, k3tog, yo, k2tog. 9 sts.
Rep last 12 rows until edging measures 63in/160cm,
ending with RS facing for bind-off.
Bind off.

TO FINISH
Weave in any yarn ends.
Lay pieces flat and gently steam work.
Place front and back together, with right sides facing
and front edge with lace panel aligned with ribbed
edge of back. Sew together three sides, leaving lace
and ribbed end open. Turn right-side out.
Sew together cast-on and bind-off edges of lace
edging.
Sew edging to pillow cover along seam line between
back and front and along open edge of front, slightly
gathering as you proceed and pinching in more fully
at each corner.
Cut cotton tape into four pieces and sew in pairs to
each side of pillow opening.
Insert pillow form and tie tapes.

BIRD MOBILE

see pages 60–63

This is a pretty play on traditional nursery decoration. Knitted silhouette birds and beads with knitted covers are assembled with shiny natural buttons, wooden beads, and silk ribbons to create a simple and inexpensive baby buggy toy or mobile.

MATERIALS

MOBILE

1 x 1¾oz/50g ball (131yd/120m per ball) of Rowan Purelife Organic Cotton DK Naturally Dyed (or a similar double-knitting-weight organic cotton yarn) in each of pink and mid blue

Pair of size 3 (3.25mm) knitting needles

1 large wooden bead 1½in/3.5cm in diameter

2 small wooden beads ½in/1cm in diameter

39in/1m of ¼in/7mm wide silk ribbon in each of pale green and pale pink

1 mother-of-pearl button ⅝in/1.5cm diameter

Approximately 5½yd/5m of hemp yarn

Wire coat hanger

BABY BUGGY TOY

1 x 1¾oz/50g ball (164yd/150m per ball) of Rowan Fine Milk Cotton (or a similar super-fine-weight cotton-blend yarn) in each of pink, barley sugar, lilac, liquorice, and turquoise

Pair of size 1 (2.25mm) knitting needles

5 large wooden beads 1¼in/3cm in diameter

8 small wooden beads ¾in/2cm in diameter

39in/1m of ¼in/7mm wide silk ribbon in each of pale peach, turquoise, and lavender

3 mother-of-pearl buttons 1in/2.5cm in diameter

Approximately 39in/1m of hemp yarn

BOTH MOBILE AND TOY

Natural organic cotton stuffing

Large-eyed blunt-ended sewing needle

Templates for the wings (see page 135)

Scraps of cotton and linen fabrics

Embroidery thread

ABBREVIATIONS

kfb knit into front and back of next stitch to increase one stitch.

See also page 139.

TIPS AND TECHNIQUES

* The birds and wooden bead covers for the mobile and baby buggy toy are worked from the same instructions, using the yarn and needles as specified above.

BIRDS

Using needles and yarn as explained in Tips and Techniques, make 4 birds for baby buggy toy and 1 for mobile as follows:

Cast on 8 sts.

Beg with a k row, work 14 rows in St st.

Row 15 K, inc 1 st at each end of row. **10 sts.**

Beg with a p row, work 9 rows in St st.

Row 25 Kfb, k2, m1, k4, m1, k1, kfb, k1. **14 sts.**

Row 26 P.

Row 27 Kfb, k3, m1, k6, m1, k2, kfb, k1. **18 sts.**

Row 28 P.

Row 29 Kfb, k4, m1, k8, m1, k3, kfb, k1. **22 sts.**

Row 30 P.

Row 31 Kfb, k5, m1, k10, m1, k4, kfb, k1. **26 sts.**

Beg with a p row, work 5 rows in St st.

Row 37 K2tog tbl, k to last 2 sts, k2tog. **24 sts.**

Row 38 P.

Row 39 K2tog tbl, k4, k2tog, k8, k2tog tbl, k4, k2tog. 20 sts.

Row 40 P.

Row 41 K2tog tbl, k3, k2tog, k6, k2tog tbl, k3, k2tog. 16 sts.

Beg with a p row, work 5 rows in St st.

Row 47 K2tog tbl, k to last 2 sts, k2tog. 14 sts.

Row 48 P.

Row 49 K2tog tbl, k to last 2 sts, k2tog. 12 sts.

Row 50 P.

Row 51 K2tog tbl, k2, k2tog, k2tog tbl, k2, k2tog. 8 sts.

Row 52 [P2tog] to end of row. 4 sts.

Row 53 K1, k2tog, k1. 3 sts.

Row 54 Sl 1, p2tog, psso.

Fasten off.

Fold in half and sew seam, stuffing as you proceed.

WOODEN BEAD COVERS

Using needles and yarn as explained in Tips and Techniques, make 5 bead covers for baby buggy toy and 1 for mobile as follows:

Cast on 11 sts.

Row 1 [Kfb] to end. 22 sts.

Beg with a p row, work 11 rows in St st.

Row 13 [K2tog] to end of row. 11 sts.

Row 14 [P2tog] to last st, p1. 6 sts.

Cut yarn leaving a very long end, thread through rem sts, pull up tightly, and secure firmly. Use long yarn end to sew side seam, then insert large wooden bead, gather up cast-on edge around bead, and secure firmly.

TO ASSEMBLE BABY BUGGY TOY

Take approximately 39in/1m of hemp yarn and make a loop at one end by tying a slip knot. Pass two ¾in/2cm wooden beads over the end, *thread on a covered bead, a button, and one ¾in/2cm wooden bead, rep from * once, **thread on a covered bead, one ¾in/2cm wooden bead, and a button, rep from ** once, thread on a covered bead, add two ¾in/2cm wooden beads, then spacing all the elements out so that the final length will be approximately 21½in/55cm, tie a slip knot at end of string.

Using the wing templates on page 135, cut one wing in fabric for each bird and stitch onto the side of the birds; then on the other side, embroider French knots or small flowers to decorate.

Take ribbon lengths and tie around birds, criss-crossing body, then attach to main string and tie in a secure bow, adjusting height away from baby.

TO ASSEMBLE MOBILE

Bend the wire coat hanger into a circle. Completely wrap the wire in narrow lengths of assorted fabrics and bind the hook of the hanger in hemp yarn.

Tie small pieces of fabric over the wrapping, then tie a ribbon bow at the base of the hook and another at the bottom of the circle.

Using the wing templates on page 135, cut two wing pieces from fabric and sew one to each side of bird and decorate with French knots.

Tie the bird to one end of a length of hemp yarn, thread on a ½in/1cm wooden bead, a button, a covered wooden bead, held on place with knots, and another ½in/1cm wooden bead, tie a knot to hold in place, then tie to the base of the hook to hang in the center of the circle.

DIAPER COVER

see pages 64–65

A traditional knitted garment for baby, which is back in vogue among today's environmentally concerned new mothers, these soaker panties are a simple diaper cover for both daytime and nighttime. Knitted in an organic cotton yarn, which is naturally antibacterial and breathable, this yarn comes in many pretty shades that are created from herb and plant dyes. The purest yarn for the softest skin.

SIZES
To fit 0–3(3–6: 6–9) months

MATERIALS
2 (2: 2) x 1¾oz/50g balls (131yd/120m per ball) of Rowan Purelife Organic Cotton DK Naturally Dyed (or a similar double-knitting-weight organic cotton yarn) in pink, green, or ecru
Pair each of sizes 3 and 5 (3mm and 3.75mm) knitting needles
Waist length of ¾in/2cm wide soft elastic
10in/25cm of ⅝in/1.5cm wide cotton tape (optional)

GAUGE
22 sts and 30 rows to 4in/10cm square over St st using size 5 (3.75mm) needles. Always work a gauge swatch and change needle size if necessary.

ABBREVIATIONS
See page 139.

BACK
*With size 5 (3.75mm) needles, cast on 19 sts.
SHAPE LEGS AND CROTCH
Beg shaping legs and crotch as follows:
Row 1 K.
Row 2 Cast on 6 sts onto left needle and p all sts.
Row 3 Cast on 6 sts onto left needle and k these 6 sts, skp, k15, k2tog, k to end.
Row 4 Cast on 6 sts onto left needle and p all sts.
Row 5 Cast on 6 sts onto left needle and k these 6 sts, k6, skp, k13, k2tog, k to end.
Row 6 Cast on 9 sts onto left needle and p all sts.
Row 7 Cast on 9 sts onto left needle and k these 9 sts, k12, skp, k11, k2tog, k to end.
Row 8 Cast on 9 sts onto left needle and p all sts.
Row 9 Cast on 9 sts onto left needle and k these 9 sts, k21, skp, k9, k2tog, k to end.
Row 10 Cast on 2 (3: 4) sts onto left needle and p all sts.
Row 11 Cast on 2 (3: 4) sts onto left needle and k these 2 (3: 4) sts, k30, skp, k7, k2tog, k to end. 73 (75: 77) sts.
Row 12 P.
Place a marker at each end of last row.
Row 13 K32 (33: 34) sts, skp, k5, k2tog, k to end.
Row 14 P.
Row 15 K32 (33: 34) sts, skp, k3, k2tog, k to end.
Row 16 P.
Row 17 K32 (33: 34) sts, skp, k1, k2tog, k to end.
Row 18 P.
Row 19 K32 (33: 34) sts, sl 1, k2tog, psso, k to end. 65 (67: 69) sts.
Row 20 P.
Work even in St st until work measures 5 (5¼: 5¾)in/12.5 (13.5: 14.5)cm from markers, ending with RS facing for next row. *

SHAPE BACK

Row 1 K56 (58: 60) sts, turn.
Row 2 P47 (49: 51) sts, turn.
Row 3 K37 (39: 41) sts, turn.
Row 4 P27 (29: 31) sts, turn.
Row 5 K17 (19: 21) sts, turn.
Row 6 P7 (9: 11) sts, turn.
Row 7 K all sts.
Row 8 P all sts.
**Change to size 3 (3mm) needles and work waistband as follows:
Work 8 rows in St st, ending with RS facing for next row.
Next row (RS) P (to make fold-line ridge).
Beg with a p row, work 7 rows in St st, ending with RS facing for next row.
Bind off all sts loosely.**

FRONT

Work as for Back from * to * and then as for Back from ** to **.

TO FINISH

Weave in any yarn ends. Gently steam work.
Sew crotch seam using mattress stitch.

LEG BANDS

With size 3 (3mm) needles and RS facing, pick up and k 64 (66: 68) sts evenly around leg shaping.
Work 5 rows in k1, p1 rib.
Bind off in rib.
Rep for other leg band.
Sew side seams.
Turn waistband to inside along ridge row and slipstitch in place, leaving a small opening.
Insert elastic and sew ends of elastic together. Sew opening closed.

If desired, make a bow from cotton tape and sew securely to front of panties.

HEIRLOOM CRIB QUILT

see pages 66–67

Treasured pieces of vintage fabric are a constant source of inspiration. Combined with ten squares of knitted lace worked in a cashmere-blend yarn, the simple embroidered cottons of yesteryear create an especially pretty and covetable crib quilt. Once assembled, the squares are backed with broderie anglaise and edged in old lace. Keep the colors in the design neutral for a timeless appeal.

SIZE
Approximately 32in/80cm x 40in/100cm, excluding edging

MATERIALS
4 x 1¾oz/50g balls (120yd/110m per ball) of Lanaknits Cashmere Canapa (or a similar double-knitting-weight cashmere/cotton-blend yarn) in ecru
Pair of size 6 (4mm) knitting needles
10 pieces of vintage (or similar) fabric, each 9in/23cm square
Lightweight iron-on interfacing
Approximately 7¾yd/7m of narrow lace
Microfilament thread
Approximately 4¼yd/3.8m of edging lace
Approximately 33in/83cm x 41in/103cm piece of sheeting for the inner layer of the quilt
Approximately 33in/83cm x 41in/103cm piece of broderie anglaise (or similar) for backing the quilt

GAUGE
22 sts and 28 rows to 4in/10cm square over St st using size 6 (4mm) needles. Always work a gauge swatch and change needle size if necessary.

ABBREVIATIONS
See page 139.

TIPS AND TECHNIQUES
* The quilt is made up of ten knitted squares and ten fabric squares.
* For neat edges on the knitted squares, slip the first stitch and work into the back of the last stitch on every row.

DIAMOND LACE SQUARES (MAKE TWO)
Cast on 39 sts and p 1 row.
Beg pattern as follows:
Row 1 (RS) *K4, yo, skp; rep from * to last 3 sts, k3.
Row 2 and every WS row P.
Row 3 K2, *k2tog, yo, k1, yo, skp, k1; rep from * to last st, k1.
Row 5 K1, k2tog, yo, *k3, yo, sl 1, k2tog, psso, yo; rep from * to last 6 sts, k3, yo, skp, k1.
Row 7 K3, *yo, sl 1, k2tog, psso, yo, k3; rep from * to end of row.
Row 9 Rep row 1.
Row 11 K1, *yo, skp, k4; rep from * to last 2 sts, yo, skp.
Row 13 K2, *yo, skp, k1, k2tog, yo, k1; rep from * to last st, k1.
Row 15 Rep row 7.
Row 17 Rep row 5.
Row 19 Rep row 11.
Row 20 P.
Last 20 rows are repeated to form pattern.
Work 50 rows in patt in total, so ending with the 10th row of 3rd repeat.
K 1 row.
Bind off.

LACY CHECKS SQUARES (MAKE TWO)

Cast on 41 sts and p 1 row.

Beg pattern as follows:

Row 1 (RS) K1, *yo, sl 1, k2tog, psso, yo, k3; rep from * to last 4 sts, yo, sl 1, k2tog, psso, yo, k1.

Row 2 and every WS row P.

Row 3 Rep row 1.

Row 5 K.

Row 7 K4, *yo, sl 1, k2tog, psso, yo, k3; rep from * to last st, k1.

Row 9 Rep row 7.

Row 11 K.

Row 12 P.

Last 12 rows are repeated to form pattern.

Work 48 rows in patt in total, so ending with the 12th row of 4th repeat.

Bind off.

STAGGERED FERN LACE SQUARES (MAKE TWO)

Cast on 44 sts and p 1 row.

Beg pattern as follows:

Row 1 (RS) K2, *p2, k9, yo, k1, yo, k3, sl 1, k2tog, psso, p2; rep from * once more, k2.

Row 2 and every WS row Purl.

Row 3 K2, *p2, k10, yo, k1, yo, k2, sl 1, k2tog, psso, p2; rep from * once more, k2.

Row 5 K2, *p2, k3tog, k4, yo, k1, yo, k3, [yo, k1] twice, sl 1, k2tog, psso, p2; rep from * once more, k2.

Row 7 K2, *p2, k3tog, k3, yo, k1, yo, k9, p2; rep from * once more, k2.

Row 9 K2, *p2, k3tog, k2, yo, k1, yo, k10, p2; rep from * once more, k2.

Row 11 K2, *p2, k3tog, [k1, yo] twice, k3, yo, k1, yo, k4, sl 1, k2tog, psso, p2; rep from * once more, k2.

Row 12 P.

Last 12 rows are repeated to form pattern.

Work 48 rows in patt in total, so ending with the 12th row of 4th repeat.

K 1 row.

Bind off.

ZIGZAG EYELETS SQUARES (MAKE TWO)

Cast on 45 sts and p 1 row.

Beg pattern as follows:

Row 1 (RS) K4, *yo, skp, k5; rep from * to last 6 sts, yo, skp, k4.

Row 2 and every WS row Purl.

Row 3 K5, *yo, skp, k5; rep from * to last 5 sts, yo, skp, k3.

Row 5 K6, *yo, skp, k5; rep from * to last 4 sts, yo, skp, k2.

Row 7 K7, *yo, skp, k5; rep from * to last 3 sts, yo, skp, k1.

Row 9 K3, *k2tog, yo, k5; rep from * to last 7 sts, k2tog, yo, k5.

Row 11 K2, *k2tog, yo, k5; rep from * to last 8 sts, k2tog, yo, k6.

Row 13 K1, *k2tog, yo, k5; rep from * to last 9 sts, k2tog, yo, k7.

Row 15 *K2tog, yo, k5; rep from * to last 10 sts, k2tog, yo, k8.

Row 16 P.

Last 16 rows are repeated to form pattern.

Work 48 rows in patt in total, so ending with the 16th row of 3rd repeat.

K 1 row.

Bind off.

LACE DIAMOND SQUARES (MAKE TWO)

Cast on 40 sts and p 1 row.

Beg pattern as follows:

Row 1 (RS) *K1, yo, k3, pass 3rd st on right-hand needle over first 2 sts; rep from * to end of row.
Row 2 and every WS row P.
Row 3 K.
Row 5 K3, *yo, skp, k6; rep from * to last 6 sts, yo, skp, k3.
Row 7 K2, *[yo, skp] twice, k4; rep from * to last 7 sts, [yo, skp] twice, k2.
Row 9 K1, *[yo, skp] 3 times, k2; rep from * to last 8 sts, [yo, skp,] 3 times, k1.
Row 11 Rep row 7.
Row 13 Rep row 5.
Row 15 K.
Row 16 P.
Last 16 rows are repeated to form pattern.
Work 52 rows in patt in total, so ending with the 4th row of 4th repeat.
Bind off.

TO FINISH
Each knitted piece should measure 8in/20cm square, so gently press each piece, easing to shape and size.
Iron interfacing onto the wrong side of each fabric square and lightly mark out the center 8in/20cm square.
The crib quilt is made up of 5 rows of 4 squares each. Arrange the knitted and fabric squares to create a good mix, the knitted squares can be placed horizontally, vertically, or reversed.
Sewing the knitted pieces directly onto the fabric pieces and using the marked 8in/20cm outlines on the fabrics as a guide, make the 5 strips of 4 squares. Sew the 5 strips together, to create the quilt top and gently press.
Lay the quilt top right side up on top of the sheeting and ease the knitted pieces into place to avoid stretching. Sew the two layers together around the outer edge, taking a ½in/1.5cm seam allowance on the sheeting and the fabric squares and stitching close to the edge on the knitted squares.
Pin the narrow lace over the seams between the squares; the fancy edge of the narrow lace should face the fabric pieces, so twist it at the corners (see diagram opposite).
Using microfilament thread, zigzag stitch the narrow lace in place.
Pin the edging lace to the right side of the cover, with the straight edge of the edging lace aligned with stitching joining the two layers and the fancy edge facing inward. While pinning, ease in extra fullness at the corners. Then machine stitch the edging lace in place.
Fold the seam allowance to the wrong side and press the edging lace so the fancy edge faces outward.
Fold under and press ½in/1.5cm to the wrong side all around the edge of the broderie anglaise backing.
With wrong sides facing, hand sew the backing to the cover. Press gently.

SPOTTY GIRAFFE

see pages 68–69

Worked in organic cotton yarn, this quirky knitted toy is embroidered with spots in a contrasting color. The added suede ears and tail give the giraffe his unique character.

SIZE
Approximately 12½in/32cm tall

MATERIALS
2 x 1¾oz/50g balls (93yd/85m per ball) of Rowan Handknit Cotton (or a similar double knitting-weight cotton yarn) in ecru (A), 1 x 1¾oz/50g ball in lilac (B), and a small amount in taupe (C)
Pair of size 5 (3.75mm) knitting needles
Natural organic cotton stuffing
Scrap of suede or felt
2 small buttons
20in/50cm of ⅝in/1.5cm wide cotton tape or ribbon
Templates for the ears and tail (see page 135)

GAUGE
22 sts and 40 rows to 4in/10cm square over St st using size 5 (3.75mm) needles. Always work a gauge swatch and change needle size if necessary.

ABBREVIATIONS
See page 139.

TIPS AND TECHNIQUES
* The giraffe is worked throughout in stockinette stitch using size 5 (3.75mm) needles.

BODY AND LEGS
* Starting with back leg and C, cast on 14 sts.
Beg with a k row, work 2 rows in St st.
Next row K2tog, k to last 2 sts, k2tog. **12 sts.**
Cont in St st throughout, work 4 rows.
Change to A.
Beg with a p row, work 9 rows.
Next row K1, m1, k to last st, m1, k1. **14 sts.**
Rep last 10 rows twice more. **18 sts.**
Beg with a p row, work 3 rows. *
Leave sts on a spare needle.
Rep from * to * for second leg.
Next row (RS) K18 from second leg, then k across 18 sts from first leg. **36 sts.**
Work 2 rows.
Next row P17 sts, m1, p2, m1, p17.
Next row K16, m1, k6, m1, k16.
Next row P15, m1, p10, m1, p15.
Cont in this way to inc 2 sts on every row, working 4 sts more between incs, until there are 60 sts.
Next row P7, p2tog, p42, p2tog, p7.
Next row K8, k2tog, k38, k2tog, k8.
Cont in this way to dec 2 sts on every row, working 1 st more before first dec and after second dec and 4 sts less between the decs, until 40 sts rem.
Beg with a p row, work 16 rows.
Next row P2tog, p to last 2 sts, p2tog.
Beg with a k row, work 13 rows.
Next row P2tog, p to last 2 sts, p2tog. **36 sts.**
Now divide for the front legs
Next row K18, turn and leave rem 18 sts on a holder.
**Beg with a p row, work 10 rows.
Next row P2tog, p to last 2 sts, p2tog.
Beg with a k row, work 7 rows.
Rep last 8 rows twice more.
Work 11 rows.

Change to C.

Work 2 rows.

Next row K2tog, k to last 2 sts, k2tog.

Work 3 rows.

Bind off.**

With RS facing, k across 18 sts on holder and rep from ** to **.

NECK

With A, cast on 30 sts.

Beg with a k row, work 5 rows in St st.

Next row P2tog, p to last 2 sts, p2tog.

Rep last 6 rows twice more.

Cont in St st throughout, work 7 rows.

Next row P2tog, p to last 2 sts, p2tog.

Work 15 rows.

Next row P2tog, p to last 2 sts, p2tog. 20 sts.

Work 18 rows. Bind off.

FRONT OF HEAD PIECES (MAKE TWO)

With A, cast on 13 sts.

Beg with a k row, work 10 rows in St st.

Next row K2tog, k to last 2 sts, k2tog.

Cont in St st throughout, work 4 rows.

Dec 1 st at each end of the next 3 rows. 5 sts.

Bind off.

TO FINISH

Weave in all yarn ends.

Lay work out flat and press under a damp cloth.

EMBROIDERY

With B, embroider French knots all over body, legs, neck, and head pieces.

ASSEMBLY

Stitch legs and underbody seams, leaving an opening for the stuffing. Stuff firmly and sew opening closed.

Bend legs to a standing position and stitch them in place to the underbody.

Sew long neck seam, leaving cast-on and bound-off edges open. Fold neck in half and stitch across bound-off edge. Stuff neck firmly and sew cast-on edge to body with neck seam at front.

Sew the two head pieces together around the edge, leaving cast-on edges open; stuff lightly and sew to top of neck.

Taking stitches through the head and pulling tightly, sew one button to each side of head for eyes.

Using the ear template on page 135, cut two pieces of suede. Pinch ear in half lengthwise and stitch securely to top of head.

Using the tail template on page 135, cut tail piece. Cut a fringe at one end, roll slightly and sew firmly in position to end of body.

Tie ribbon around neck and trim ends.

AFTERCARE

Sponge with a wet cloth, hand wash, or wash in a washing machine on a delicate cycle at a low temperature.

NIGHTIE AND HAT

see pages 72–75

S nug, practical, and made in fine
natural cotton in stockinette stitch,
this outfit is perfect for even the
smallest baby. It is a modern take on the
classic newborn layette. The nightie has an
envelope neck, integral scratch mittens, and
an easy-open snap hem.

SIZES
To fit newborn (0–3: 3–6) months
NIGHTIE
Knitted chest measurement 18½ (20: 22)in/46 (50:
55)cm
Length to shoulder 19 (20½: 23)in/48 (52: 58)cm
Sleeve length 6 (6¾: 7½)in/15 (17: 19)cm

MATERIALS
5 x 1¾oz/50g balls (186yd/170m per ball) of Rowan
4-Ply Cotton (or a similar super-fine-weight cotton
yarn) in cream or shale
Pair each of sizes 2 and 3 (3mm and 3.25mm)
knitting needles
6in/15cm of ⅝in/1.5cm wide cotton tape
4 mother-of-pearl buttons ½in/1cm in diameter
for nightie and hat
4 mother-of-pearl buttons ¾in/2cm in diameter
for nightie
4 snaps for nightie

GAUGE
27 sts and 36 rows to 4in/10cm square over St st
using size 3 (3.25mm) needles. Always work a gauge
swatch and change needle size if necessary.

ABBREVIATIONS
See page 139.

TIPS AND TECHNIQUES
* Work fully fashioned increases as follows:
K3, m1, k to last 3 sts, m1, k3.
* Work fully fashioned decreases as follows:
On a k row—k3, k2tog, k to last 5 sts, k2tog tbl, k3.
On a p row—p3, p2tog tbl, p to last 5 sts, p2tog, p3.

NIGHTIE

BACK
With size 2 (3mm) needles, cast on 92 (100: 108) sts
and beg with a k row, work 11 rows in St st.
Next row (WS) K (to form fold-line ridge for hem).
Change to size 3 (3.25mm) needles.
Beg with a k row, cont in St st, dec 1 st (see note
on fully fashioned decreases) at each end of
13th row and every following 8th row until 62 (68:
74) sts rem.
Cont in St st throughout, work even until Back
measures 15¾ (17: 19)in/40 (43: 48)cm from fold
line, ending with RS facing for next row.
SHAPE ARMHOLES
Bind off 2 sts at beg of next 2 rows. **58 (64: 70) sts.**
Dec 1 st (see note on fully fashioned decreases) at
each end of next row and every foll alt row until
52 (58: 64) sts rem.**
Work even until armholes measure 3¼ (3½: 4)in/
8 (9: 10)cm, ending with WS facing for next row.
SHAPE ENVELOPE NECK
Next row (WS) P20 (21: 22) sts, turn and leave rem
sts on a holder.
Bind off 3 sts at neck edge on next row and foll 2 alt

rows, placing marker at armhole edge of last row. 11 (12: 13) sts.

Dec 1 st at neck edge on every row, **and at the same time** inc 1 st (see note on fully fashioned increases) at armhole edge on every foll 3rd row until 4 incs have been worked. 3 (4: 5) sts.

Dec 1 st at neck edge on next row.

Bind off rem 2 (3: 4) sts.

With WS facing, slip center 12 (16: 20) sts onto a holder, rejoin yarn to rem sts and p to end of row.

Complete to match first side, reversing shaping.

FRONT

Work as for Back to **.

Work even until armhole measures 1½ (2: 2¼)in/ 4 (5: 6)cm, ending with WS facing for next row.

SHAPE ENVELOPE NECK

Next row (WS) P21 (24: 27) sts, turn and leave rem sts on a holder.

Dec 1 st (see note on fully fashioned decreases) at neck edge on every row until 19 (18: 17) sts rem, then on next row and every foll alt row until 11 (12: 13) sts rem. Work even for 2 rows, placing marker at armhole edge of last row.

Dec 1 st at neck edge on every row, **and at the same time** inc 1 st at armhole edge on every foll 3rd row until 4 incs have been worked. 3 (4: 5) sts.

Dec 1 st at neck edge on next row.

Bind off.

With WS facing, slip center 10 sts onto a holder, rejoin yarn to rem sts and p to end of row.

Complete to match first side, reversing shaping.

SLEEVES WITH SCRATCH MITTENS

With size 3 (3.25mm) needles, cast on 16 sts.

Work 2 rows in k1, p1 rib.

Beg with a k row, work 13 rows in St st, ending with WS facing for next row.

Change to size 2 (3mm) needles.

Next 2 rows Cast on 9 (10: 11) sts onto left needle and work in k1, p1 rib across all sts. 34 (36: 38) sts.

Place a marker at each end of last row.

Change to size 3 (3.25mm) needles.

Beg with a k row, work in St st, inc 1 st (see note on fully fashioned increases) at each end of 5th row and every foll 6th row until there are 50 (54: 58) sts.

Cont in St st throughout, work even until sleeve measures 6 (6¾: 7½)in/15 (17: 19)cm from markers, ending with RS facing for next row.

SHAPE TOP OR SLEEVE

Bind off 2 sts at beg of next 2 rows. 46 (50: 54) sts.

Dec 1 st at each end of next row and every foll alt row until 34 (38: 42) sts rem.

P 1 row.

Bind off loosely.

FRONT NECKBAND

With size 2 (3mm) needles and RS facing, pick up and k 33 (35: 37) sts along right neck, k across 10 sts from holder, and pick up and k 33 (35: 37) sts up left neck. 76 (80: 84) sts.

Work 3 rows in k1, p1 rib.

Bind off in rib.

BACK NECKBAND

With size 2 (3mm) needles and RS facing, pick up and k 24 (25: 26) sts along right neck, k across 12 (16: 20) sts from holder, and pick up and k 24 (25: 26) sts up left neck. 60 (66: 72) sts.

Work 3 rows in k1, p1 rib.

Bind off in rib.

TO FINISH
Weave in any yarn ends.
Lay work out flat and gently steam.
Place the back over the front, matching markers at armhole edge, and sew in place to make the envelope neck.
Sew sleeves into armholes, easing to fit.
Fold scratch mitten flap up onto right side of sleeve and sew in place at sides.
Sew sleeve seams.
Fold back and front along fold line and slipstitch hem in place.
Sew side seams from top of hem to armhole.
Sew large snaps to wrong side of hem, evenly spaced, then sew large buttons to right side of front over snaps.
Cut a short length of cotton tape, tie in the center, and sew to center front, or sew two small buttons to center front.

HAT

TO MAKE
With size 2 (3mm) needles, cast on 78 (88: 98) sts.
Work 1½in/4cm in k1, p1 rib, inc 0 (1: 2) sts at center of last row. 78 (89: 100) sts.
Change to size 3 (3.25mm) needles.
Beg with a k row, work in St st until work measures 3in/7.5cm from cast-on edge, ending with RS facing for next row.
Next row (RS) K1, [k2tog, k5 (6: 7)] to end of row. 67 (78: 89) sts.
Cont in St st throughout, work 3 rows.
Next row K1, [k2tog, k4 (5: 6)] to end of row. 56 (67: 78) sts.
Work 3 rows.

Next row K1, [k2tog, k3 (4: 5)] to end of row. 45 (56: 67) sts.
Work 3 rows.
Next row K1, [k2tog, k2 (3: 4)] to end of row. 34 (45: 56) sts.
Work 1 (3: 3) rows.
Next row K1, [k2tog, k1 (2: 3)] to end of row. 23 (34: 45) sts.
Work 1 (1: 3) rows.
2ND AND 3RD SIZES ONLY
Next row K1, [k2tog, k– (1: 2)] to end of row. – (23: 34) sts.
Work 1 row.
3RD SIZE ONLY
Next row K1, [k2tog, k– (–: 1)] to end of row. – (–: 23) sts.
Work 1 row.
ALL SIZES
Next row K1, [k2tog] to end of row. 12 sts.
Work 1 row.
Next row [K2tog] to end of row. 6 sts.
Cut yarn, thread through rem sts, pull up tightly, and secure firmly.

TO FINISH
Weave in any yarn ends.
Lay work out flat and gently steam.
Sew seam.
Cut a short length of cotton tape, tie in the center, and sew in place above ribbing on hat as shown, or sew on two small buttons.

TEMPLATES

TEDDY BEAR
see pages 80–83

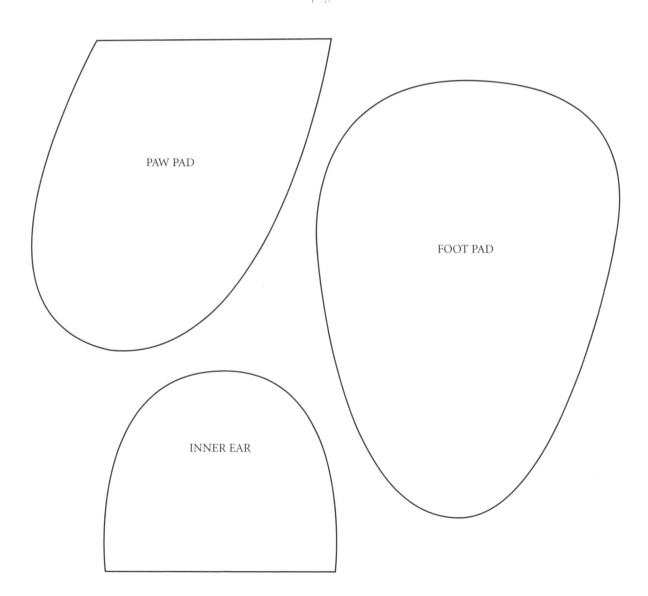

PAW PAD

FOOT PAD

INNER EAR

BIRD MOBILE

see pages 120–121

SPOTTY GIRAFFE

see pages 128–129

LARGE WING

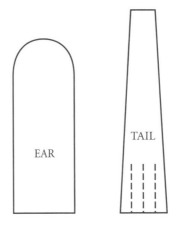

EAR

TAIL

SMALL WING

RECOMMENDED YARNS

The following is a list of the yarns used in this book. Although I have recommended a specific yarn for each project, you can use substitutes if you prefer. If you decide to use an alternative, purchase a substitute that is as close as possible to the original yarn in thickness, weight, and texture so it will work with the pattern instructions. Buy only one ball to start with, so you can test the effect. Calculate the number of balls you need by yardage rather than weight. The recommended knitting-needle size and gauge on the yarn labels are extra guides to the yarn thickness. To obtain Lanaknits, R.E. Dickie British Breeds, Rowan, and Yeoman's yarns, go to the websites below for mail-order or to find a store in your area:

www.lanaknits.com / www.hempforknitting.com
www.britishwool.com
www.knitrowan.com
www.yeoman-yarns.co.uk

LANAKNITS ALLHEMP6
A double-knitting-weight hemp yarn; 100% hemp; 165yd/150m per 3½oz/100g skein; recommended gauge—22 sts x 28 rows per 4in/10cm over St st using size 5 (3.75mm) needles.

LANAKNITS CASHMERE CANAPA
A double-knitting-weight cashmere/cotton-blend yarn; 60% cotton, 30% cashmere, 10% hemp; 120yd/110m per 50g ball; recommended gauge—22 sts x 34 rows per 4in/10cm over St st using size 5 (3.75mm) needles.

R.E. DICKIE BRITISH BREEDS ARAN WEIGHT NATURAL
An aran-weight wool yarn; 100% wool; 131yd/120m per 3½oz/100g; recommended gauge—18 sts per 4in/10cm over St st using size 8 (5mm) needles.

ROWAN CLASSIC (RYC) BABY ALPACA DK
A double-knitting-weight alpaca yarn; 100% baby alpaca; 109yd/100m per 1¾oz/50g; recommended gauge—22 sts x 30 rows per 4in/10cm over St st using size 6 (4mm) needles.

ROWAN CLASSIC (RYC) BAMBOO SOFT
A double-knitting-weight bamboo yarn; 100% bamboo; 112yd/102m per 1¾oz/50g; recommended gauge—25 sts x 30 rows per 4in/10cm over St st using size 5 (3.75mm) needles.

ROWAN 4-PLY COTTON
A super-fine-weight cotton yarn; 100% cotton; 186yd/170m per 1¾oz/50g; recommended gauge—27–29 sts x 37–39 rows per 4in/10cm over St st using size 2–3 (3–3.25mm) needles.

ROWAN HANDKNIT COTTON
A double-knitting-weight cotton yarn; 100% cotton; 93yd/85m per 1¾oz/50g; recommended gauge—19–20 sts x 28 rows per 4in/10cm over St st using size 6–7 (4–4.5mm) needles.

ROWAN MILK COTTON—DK
A double-knitting-weight cotton-blend yarn; 70% cotton, 30% milk protein; 124yd/113m per 1¾oz/50g; recommended gauge—22 sts x 30 rows per 4in/10cm over St st using size 5 (3.75mm) needles.

ROWAN MILK COTTON—FINE
A super-fine-weight cotton-blend yarn; 70% cotton, 30% milk protein; 164yd/150m per 1¾oz/50g; recommended gauge—30 sts x 38 rows per 4in/10cm over St st using size 2 (2.75mm) needles.

ROWAN PURELIFE ORGANIC COTTON DK NATURALLY DYED
A double-knitting-weight organic cotton yarn; 100% organic cotton; 131yd/120m per 1¾oz/50g; recommended gauge—22 sts x 30 rows per 4in/10cm over St st using size 5 (3.75mm) needles.

ROWAN PURELIFE BRITISH SHEEP BREEDS UNDYED
An aran-weight pure wool yarn; 100% wool; 120yd/110m per 3½oz/100g; recommended gauge—13 sts x 18 rows per 4in/10cm over St st using size 10½ (7mm) needles.

YEOMAN'S COTTON CANNELE 4-PLY
A super-fine-weight mercerized cotton yarn; 100% cotton; 957yd/850m per 8½oz/245g cone; recommended gauge—33 sts x 44 rows per 4in/10cm over St st using size 2 (2.75mm) needles.

PATTERN INFORMATION

Each garment is given in three different sizes, ranging from newborn up to 6 or 9 months. The smallest size is given first and appears outside the parentheses. The larger sizes are given inside the parentheses in ascending order. When working through the instructions, your size will be in the same position throughout the pattern. If only one number is given, it applies to all three of the sizes and where 0 (or –) appears no stitches or rows are worked for this size. To avoid any confusion, highlight the relevant instructions for your size within the pattern. Where instructions are given in brackets [ ] or between asterisks, work these instructions the number of time stated after the brackets or asterisk.

ABBREVIATIONS

All knitting patterns follow a basic structure and use the same standard abbreviations and terminology.

alt	alternate
beg	begin(ning)
cm	centimeter(s)
cont	continu(e)(ing)
dec	decreas(e)(ing)
foll	follow(s)(ing)
g	gram(s)
garter st	garter stitch (k every row)
in	inch(es)
inc	increas(e)(ing)
k	knit
LH	left hand
m	meter(s)
m1	make one stitch by picking up horizontal loop before next stitch and working into back of it
mm	millimeter(s)
p	purl
patt	pattern
psso	pass slipped stitch over
rem	remain(s)(ing)
rep	repeat(ing)
rev St st	reverse stockinette stitch (p all RS rows, k all WS rows)
RH	right hand
RS	right side
skp	slip 1, knit 1, pass slipped stitch over (one stitch decreased)
sl	slip
st(s)	stitch(es)
St st	stockinette stitch (k all RS rows, p all WS rows)
tbl	through back of loop(s)
tog	together
WS	wrong side
yd	yard(s)
yo	yarn over right needle to make a new stitch

GARMENT CARE

When you invest so much time in creating a hand-knitted garment, great care should be taken in the laundering of these items. How frequent a garment needs washing depends on how it is worn, but children's clothes often need laundering on a regular basis. The yarn you use must be able to stand up to this, but this does not necessarily mean that all yarns must be machine washable. Look at the labels: those on most commercial yarns have instructions for washing or dry cleaning, drying, and pressing. So, for a project knitted in one yarn only, a quick look at the yarn label will tell you how to care for it. If you wish to work with several yarns in one piece of work, the aftercare requires a little more thought. If one label suggests dry cleaning, then be sure to dry clean the garment.

WASHING

If in doubt about whether or not your knitting is washable, then make a little swatch of the yarn. Wash this to see if the fabric is affected by being immersed in water or not, watching for shrinkage and stretching. If you are satisfied with the results, go ahead and wash the knitting by hand in lukewarm water. Never use hot water, as this will felt your fabric, and you will not be able to return it to its prewashed state. In particular, wool tends to react to major changes in temperature.

When washing any knitted item, handle it carefully. There should be enough water to cover the garment completely and the soap should be thoroughly dissolved before immersing it. If you need to sterlize any garment that has become badly soiled or stained, then use a proprietary brand of sterilizer for this purpose. As a precaution, test wash any trims you use before you make up the garment with them. Nothing is more infuriating than to spoil an entire garment because the trim colors run in the wash. Natural fibers such as wool, cotton and silk are usually better washed by hand, and in pure soap, than in a machine. However, should you decide to wash any knitted garment in a washing machine, place it inside a pillowslip as an extra precaution. Soap flakes are kinder to sensitive skins than most detergents, provided all traces of the soap are removed in the rinsing process.

RINSING

Squeeze out any excess water, never wring it out. Rinse thoroughly, until every trace of soap is removed, as any left in will mat the fibers and may irritate the skin. Use at least two changes of water or continue until the water is clear and without soap bubbles. Take care, too, to keep the rinsing water the same temperature as the washing water.

SPINNING

The garments can be rinsed on a short rinse and spin as part of the normal washing machine cycle for delicate fabrics. Again, as an extra precaution, place the item to be spun inside a pillowslip.